D0713890

SOCIAL SOLIDARITY AND THE GIFT

This book brings together two traditions of thinking about social ties: sociological theory on solidarity and anthropological theory on gift exchange. The
purpose of the book is to explore how both theoretical traditions may complete and enrich each other, and how they may illuminate transformations
in solidarity. The main argument, supported by empirical illustrations, is
that a theory of solidarity should incorporate some of the core insights from
anthropological gift theory. The book presents a theoretical model covering
both positive and negative – selective and excluding – aspects and consequences of solidarity. It is concluded that over the past century solidarity
has undergone a fundamental transformation, from Durkheim's "organic"
solidarity to a type of solidarity that can be called "segmented": separate,
autonomous social segments connecting with other segments, no longer out
of necessity and mutual dependency but on the basis of individual choice.
Solidarity has, thereby, become more noncommittal.

Aafke E. Komter is Professor of Social Science occupying the endowed chair of
Comparative Studies of Social Solidarity of Utrecht University, and Head of
the Department of Social Science at University College, Utrecht. Her articles
on informal giving, reciprocity and solidarity, power, morality, and gender
issues have appeared in international journals such as *Sociology*, the *Journal
of Marriage and the Family*, and the *Journal of Family Issues*. She is editor of
The Gift: An Interdisciplinary Perspective.

Social Solidarity and the Gift

AAFKE E. KOMTER

Utrecht University

CAMBRIDGE
UNIVERSITY PRESS

PUBLISHED BY THE PRESS SYNDICATE OF THE UNIVERSITY OF CAMBRIDGE
The Pitt Building, Trumpington Street, Cambridge, United Kingdom

CAMBRIDGE UNIVERSITY PRESS
The Edinburgh Building, Cambridge CB2 2RU, UK
40 West 20th Street, New York, NY 10011-4211, USA
477 Williamstown Road, Port Melbourne, VIC 3207, Australia
Ruiz de Alarcón 13, 28014 Madrid, Spain
Dock House, The Waterfront, Cape Town 8001, South Africa

http://www.cambridge.org

© Cambridge University Press 2005

This book is in copyright. Subject to statutory exception
and to the provisions of relevant collective licensing agreements,
no reproduction of any part may take place without
the written permission of Cambridge University Press.

First published 2005

Printed in the United States of America

Typeface Minion 10.5/15 pt.   *System* LATEX 2$_\varepsilon$ [TB]

A catalog record for this book is available from the British Library.

Library of Congress Cataloging in Publication Data

Komter, Aafke E.
Social solidarity and the gift / Aafke E. Komter.
     p.   cm.
Includes bibliographical references and index.
ISBN 0-521-84100-3 (hardback) – ISBN 0-521-60084-7 (pbk.)
1. Gifts.   2. Solidarity.   3. Generosity.   I. Title.
GT3040.K66   2004
394–dc22   2004045809

ISBN 0 521 84100 3 hardback
ISBN 0 521 60084 7 paperback

Contents

Contents

Contents

Preface

This book is the result of more than ten years of research and teaching about the themes of the gift and solidarity. It all started in 1992 when, in conversations with anthropologist Willy Jansen, I was put on the track of the gift literature. This was followed by an invitation from the Dutch newspaper *Trouw* on the occasion of its fiftieth anniversary to conduct a study into gift giving in the Netherlands, together with the sociologist Kees Schuyt. The theme proved not only interesting because of its interdisciplinarity and theoretical richness but also surprisingly mundane and amusing. Suddenly it was less sinking to be asked about "your work": everybody gives gifts to others, and everybody has something to tell about totally wrong gifts received or about dubious motives to give a gift to another person. During the second half of the 1990s a remarkable development occurred in the political tide in Holland: after having led a hidden existence during several decades, the themes of solidarity and social cohesion suddenly came to be exposed in full daylight. A broadly felt concern about the current state of social cohesion and solidarity in our society gave rise to extensive political and public debate. Policy documents were written and plans were made to counter the perceived threat of a dissolving community and diminished citizenship. Both the Dutch government and the Dutch Council of Scientific Research reserved money for research in the field of social cohesion and solidarity.

From the beginning the connection between my previous research theme of the gift and that of cohesion and solidarity had been clear to me. For had the classical anthropologists not convincingly argued that gifts confirm social ties and that the theory of the gift is a theory on human solidarity? Extension of my former theme to that of cohesion and solidarity was therefore a logical step. In my teaching I started to incorporate the classical and modern theories on social solidarity, and as of 2001 I became a co-researcher in a large-scale study about family solidarity, the Netherlands Kinship Panel Study, financed by the Dutch Council of Scientific Research. One question, however, had become more and more pressing over the years: why are there so few theoretical connections and crosswise references between the gift theory and theories on solidarity, when it is clear as sunlight that both concern the coming into being and the maintenance of social community? This question is central to this book.

During a couple of delightful holidays in a Breton seaside hamlet the job has been accomplished. This would not have been possible without the help of a number of colleagues and other people who offered their views and suggestions for improvement. I want to thank Jack Burgers, Louk Hagendoorn, Mirjam van Leer, Maarten Prak, and Wilma Vollebergh for their critical reading of former versions of Chapters 8 and 9. I am also grateful to Godfried Engbersen for his help in finding a suitable terminology to describe the transformation of solidarity since the late nineteenth century. The anonymous readers for Cambridge University Press have been an enormous help, and I appreciate their careful reading and invaluable suggestions. Finally, I am very grateful to Paul Verhey for his interest, patience, and continuous friendship, both in the Breton hamlet and elsewhere.

Several of the chapters of this book have been published previously. They have been brought together here with the explicit purpose of creating one coherent whole that is more than the sum of its parts. Here follows the acknowledgment of the origins of the various chapters. A former version of Chapter 1 has been published as "Heirlooms, Nikes and bribes: Towards a sociology of things," *Sociology* 35 (2001): 59–75. A former, Dutch version of Chapter 2 has been published as "De psychologie van de gift. Over geven, vergeven en vergif" [The psychology of the gift: About giving, forgiving and poison], *Psychologie & Maatschappij* 65 (1993): 306–319. A slightly different version of Chapter 3 has been published as "Gratitude and gift exchange," in R. Emmons and M. McCullough (eds.), *The Psychology of Gratitude* (New York: Oxford University Press, 2004), pp. 195–212. A former version of Chapter 4 has been published as "Women, gifts and power," in A. Komter (ed.), *The Gift: An Interdisciplinary Perspective* (Amsterdam: Amsterdam University Press, 1996), pp. 119–132. A former, Dutch version of Chapter 5 has been published as chapter 2 in A. Komter, J. Burgers, and G. Engbersen, *Het cement van de samenleving. Een verkennende studie naar solidariteit en cohesie* [The cement of society: An exploratory study of solidarity and cohesion] (Amsterdam: Amsterdam University Press, 2000), pp. 26–42. Parts of Chapter 6 have been published as "The disguised rationality of solidarity," *Journal of Mathematical Sociology* 25 (2001): 385–401; and as "Reciprocity as a principle of exclusion: Gift giving in the Netherlands," *Sociology* 30 (1996): 299–316. Parts of Chapter 7 have been published in A. Komter and W. Vollebergh, "Solidarity in Dutch families: Family ties under strain?" *Journal of Family Issues* 23 (2) (2002): 171–189. Chapters 8 and 9 have served as the basis of my inaugural speech "Solidarity and sacrifice," Utrecht University, January 2003.

Introduction

More profound insights into the nature of solidarity and trust
can be expected from applying the theory of the gift to ourselves.

(Mary Douglas 1990: xv)

Is there a similarity between giving a birthday present and doing volunteer
work? Between donating blood and being a union member? In short: what
do gifts and social solidarity have in common? Giving to a beggar or to
charity is an act of solidarity. When we are giving care or help to our
elderly parents, we are demonstrating social solidarity; at the same time
we are giving a (nonmaterial) gift to another person. The term solidarity,
apart from its ideological use, for instance in the socialist and communist
jargon, and apart from its normative commonsense use by humanitarian
organizations, political parties, or the church, has traditionally been used
in a descriptive and analytic way, with the sociological approach of Emile
Durkheim providing the first scientific attempt at theory development.

Solidarity derives from the Latin *solidare* – to make firm, to combine
parts to form a strong whole. In contrast to the term solidarity, the word
gift has an agonistic origin: the German *Gift* came from the Greek *dosis*
and Latin *dos*, which had replaced the former *venenum* because of the need
for a euphemism. Whereas solidarity is an abstract concept that remains
abstract even in its most common uses (one dictionary explanation of
solidarity is, for instance, a feeling of togetherness and willingness to take

1

the consequences of that), gift giving is often associated with concrete and material objects exchanged on certain occasions between people having a certain type of relationship to each other. This difference in abstraction level may be one explanation of the fact that the scientific histories of the concepts of solidarity and the gift have remained separate to a large extent. Also the concept of solidarity may take very concrete shape, as the preceding example demonstrates. Inversely, the concept of the gift does not exclusively indicate certain material acts but has a wealth of cultural, social, and psychological meanings as well, all referring to the abstract, symbolic functions of gift giving. Despite their differing etymological and scientific histories, both concepts are clearly related in their most fundamental and characteristic manifestations and functions. Giving gifts is an act that creates and maintains social ties by making people feel mutually obliged to give in return. Similarly, social solidarity is regarded as the glue that keeps people together, whether by mutually identifying and sharing certain norms and values, or by contributing to some common good, or both.

As Mary Douglas argues in her foreword to the translation of Mauss's *Essai sur le don* (1990 [1923]), the theory of the gift is a theory of human solidarity. Both theories – or, better, theoretical traditions – have as their main subject the way social ties come into existence and are maintained, in brief, "the problem of social order," as Talcott Parsons called it. Given their common subject matter it is surprising that both sets of theories do not seem to have influenced each other in any significant way. On the one hand, there is the anthropological and sociological tradition of thinking about the gift and reciprocity, with authors such as Malinowski, Simmel, Mauss, Lévi-Strauss, Gouldner, and Sahlins. On the other hand stands the sociological tradition of theories on solidarity and social order, in particular the work of Durkheim, Weber, and Parsons. Where there is some influence, it tends to take the form of a critical stance, for example, Gouldner's criticism of the functionalist approach within social theory, or Mauss's radicalization of Durkheim's views on the basis of social order.

Not immediately clear are how the theory of the gift and that of solidarity relate to each other, what the similarities and the differences are, and in which respects they may complete or enrich each other. Also, with regard to empirical research both traditions are rather unconnected. The bulk of empirical studies on gift giving are from non-Western societies, although in recent years some "westernization" of the research has taken place. Empirical research into solidarity has been scarce; its main focus is on attitudes toward certain forms of solidarity (e.g., state support of the socially weak, distribution of health care in view of risky life-styles). Besides some national surveys about volunteer work and money donations, and the research done within the Dutch tradition of theoretical sociology (mainly inspired by rational choice theory), there have been very few attempts to research concrete instances of solidary behavior.

During the past decade several scholarly works on the respective themes of the gift and of solidarity have appeared. In *L'esprit du don* (1992), for instance, Jacques Godbout analyzes the continuity between the "archaic" and the modern gift. Between the various types of gift – "normal" gifts, Christmas gifts, blood or organ donation, giving help to unknown people – there are interesting similarities connecting them to the gifts given in archaic society. Outside the sphere of the market, our society is still firmly rooted in a system of gift exchange. It is impossible to think of a society without gifts being circulated: gifts still create and maintain social bonds, thereby continually contributing to the revitalization of society. Some years later Maurice Godelier published *The Enigma of the Gift* (1999 [1996]) in which he reopens the anthropological debate on the meanings and functions of gift giving for the constitution of social ties and community. Returning to the classical works by Marcel Mauss and others, he tries to disentangle the enigmas that kept surrounding the gift in the eyes of many anthropologists. Drawing on the work of the late Annette Weiner, he shows that a certain category of objects can be given and kept simultaneously. Particularly objects deriving their meaning from birth, death, ancestors, or sacred powers, and which are therefore associated with human as well as cultural reproduction, are given as well as kept at the same time: their ownership is inalienable in the end, while the right of usage may be passed on to others. Another interesting publication is *The Sociology of Giving* (1999) by the German sociologist-anthropologist Helmuth Berking. Like Godbout he compares present-day giving with gift exchange in "traditional" societies and also arrives at the conclusion that giving and taking are elementary activities upon which the building of community still rests. In addition to examining the motives, occasions, and emotional norms of gift giving, he explores the historical, symbolic, and linguistic roots of the moral vocabulary related to gift giving. The concepts of hospitality, sacrifice, and gratitude are important elements in this vocabulary.

A recent publication is the interdisciplinary collection of essays edited by Mark Osteen, *The Question of the Gift* (2002). The volume comprises contributions from anthropology, literary criticism, economics, philosophy, and classics and poses questions such as: what is the role of noncommercial gift exchange in creating communities, how do people deal with objects outside the sphere of consumption, what is the relationship between gifts and commodities, to what extent are artworks gifts, is a really free gift possible or desirable? Important elements in the book are the concepts of power and reciprocity, and ample attention is given to the ethical foundations of kinship, generosity, and gratitude. Osteen feels that a too strong emphasis on (calculating) reciprocity and the implicitly economic assumptions of classical gift theory underestimate the spontaneous and sometimes altruistic character of the gift. He thus takes a stance that is contrary to Mauss's classical view that in the end every gift is based on the principle of *do ut des* (I give so that you give in return). Remarkably the book's index does not contain any reference to solidarity; although Durkheim does figure in the book a number of times, his theory on social solidarity is not mentioned.

Recent publications on solidarity are of a somewhat different nature: more conceptual and theoretical, and frequently inspired by political, social, and moral philosophy. Their point of departure is often normative: what future is left for solidarity, how can we conceptualize it in such a way that it fits our modernized society? A German collection of essays edited by Kurt Bayertz (1998), for instance, examines the moral and historical context of solidarity, in addition to offering perspectives from psychology and biology. Solidarity is also analyzed as a social norm and a civil right. Chapters on international solidarity and solidarity in the (post)modern society are included in the volume as well. In another German study that is mainly conceptual as well, Rainer Zoll (2000) discusses the juridical and French origins of the concept. He traces the conceptual history of solidarity and attempts to draw up the balance of contemporary social solidarity, in particular worker solidarity, and some new forms of solidarity in our society. He agrees with Habermas's normative conception of solidarity as tied to justice. In Zoll's view a critical test for a new conception of solidarity would be the way it would deal with our relationship to strangers.

In the Netherlands some studies have appeared that exhibit the same theoretical and conceptual concern as the German publications. The volume edited by de Wit and Manschot (1999), for instance, offers a critical reconstruction of the traditional ways of conceptualizing solidarity. The authors reflect upon how the ethical components of solidarity can still be of value to our modern democratic societies. They present theoretical arguments that connect solidarity to cosmopolitism, tolerance, and the acceptance of cultural minorities. From the perspective of the law Dorien Pessers (1999) offers an interesting analysis of the concept of reciprocity, which she considers an essential aspect of solidarity. In her interdisciplinary study she examines what this concept might mean for the various domains of law.

A British study by Turner and Rojek (2001), finally, attempts to clarify how (post)modern society deals with the principles of scarcity, on the one hand, and solidarity, on the other. This study not only offers an overview of existing social scientific theories on solidarity but also presents a normative view on the way solidarity might be given shape in a modern society.

In the present book I attempt to bring together two rather unrelated traditions of social scientific thinking about social ties: sociological theory on solidarity and anthropological theory on the cultural and social meanings of gift exchange. The purpose is to explore how both theoretical traditions may complete and enrich each other, and how these combined insights may illuminate manifestations of contemporary solidarity. The book's main argument is that a theory of solidarity could gain significantly from incorporating some of the core insights from the theoretical and empirical work on the gift. This theoretical argument is supported by empirical illustrations drawn from research on gift giving and on various forms of solidarity.

The book consists of three parts. The focus of Part I is on the socio-cultural, social-psychological, and gendered meanings of gift exchange. Chapter 1 starts at the most concrete level by investigating the trajectories of things that pass between people and the different types of meaning things become invested with as a consequence of their circulation between people. In turn, these meanings can explain how things come to play a role in gift exchange and, by that means, in creating social ties. We are strongly inclined to regard things as mute and inert. In many anthropological and sociological writings "mute" commodities are opposed to gifts, which are supposed to have a "spirit" and to have rich symbolic and social meanings. However, things also have "social lives" that bestow them with symbolic value. While things derive their symbolic meaning from exchange, the continuation of exchange is guaranteed by means of the symbolic meanings of things. This chapter investigates the social meanings of things by distinguishing four fundamental models of people's relationships to each other and to things; these models have affection, power, equality, and utility as their respective bases. Empirical research data on gift giving are used to illustrate the models.

The different patterns of giving and receiving and the meanings of things-as-gifts are further explored in Chapters 2, 3, and 4. Chapter 2 presents some empirical data on social and psychological patterns of giving and receiving. Dutch research shows a strong relationship between giving and receiving: doing well has its reward. Apparently the principle of reciprocity also applies to Western society. In addition to its social and cultural meanings the theme of the gift has great social-psychological significance. The main psychological functions of gift giving are, first, the creation of a moral bond between giver and recipient and, second, the maintenance (or disturbance) of this bond. Gifts as "tie signs" disclose the nature of the tie between giver and recipient. They reveal how we perceive the recipient while at the same time showing something about our own identity. In gift giving a range of psychological motives may be involved, varying from the desire to express love, gratitude, and friendship, to motives related to insecurity and anxiety, and to the conscious or unconscious need to offend, insult, or exploit another person. Gifts may be deceptive insofar as their manifest and latent intentions do not coincide. Empirical illustrations of offensive and embarrassing gifts are also presented. Participants in reciprocal gift exchange are involved in a psychological balance of debt, which should never be in complete equilibrium. Someone has to remain in debt toward the other, but both parties may have different ideas on the magnitude of the debt and on how long it can last. The debt balance is therefore a source of relational risks.

Gratitude is the subject of Chapter 3. According to anthropologists one of the main characteristics of the gift is that it should "move": gifts should be given and reciprocated. If a gift is kept too long, the recipient will develop a bad reputation. Gifts are not inactive but possess something of the original giver. This "spirit of the gift" wants to return to its place of origin; only then is the gift cycle completed and can a new cycle be set in motion. Gifts can only bear fruit if people show their gratitude in a proper way through passing the gift along. Gratitude may also be considered from a psychological point of view – as a moral virtue, a personality characteristic, or asset. It is something one has to learn, and some people are better equipped to learn it than others. The quality of the earliest contact with the primary caring figure seems to be at the basis of the capacity to feel and to express gratitude. A sociological view stresses gratitude as part of the chain of reciprocity, or "the moral memory of mankind," as Simmel called it. As such, gratitude fulfills important cohesive functions for society. A culture or society deprived of all acts of gratitude will inevitably break down. Issues of power and dependence may complicate gratitude. Only in more or less balanced relationships can gratitude unfold the best of its powers.

In Chapter 4 the gendered meanings of gift giving are discussed. Although Malinowski recognizes that women have a prominent role in certain ceremonial actions, he does not mention any active female part in gift exchange; all his examples are from men. Lévi-Strauss discusses the practice occurring in many non-Western societies of exchanging women as "the supreme gift." The exchange of women as marriage partners is supposed to be at the base of systems of kinship relations and thereby forms the structural fundament of culture and society as such. More recent work of Strathern and Weiner suggests that women's role in gift giving is not restricted to being merely the object of exchange but that they have an important and autonomous part in gift exchange. Empirical studies in Western society demonstrate that women, far from being passive and insignificant, play a prominent role in gift exchange: they not only give more gifts than men – material as well as nonmaterial ones – but they are also the greatest recipients. Women's gift giving seems to be caught in a paradox. On the one hand, gift exchange is a powerful means of creating social relationships and affirming ties; on the other, by giving too much, women incur the risk of losing their own identities, given their unequal societal and economic power compared with that of men.

In Part II the theories on gift giving and solidarity are brought together and their strengths and weaknesses compared. Chapter 5 examines how the theory of the gift can be connected to that of human solidarity. Classical sociologists such as Durkheim, Weber, and Parsons highlight the affective, normative, and instrumental foundations of social ties and solidarity: people come to share norms regulating their interactions and transactions, but they also develop functional relations based on more instrumental and self-interested concerns. In the work of classical anthropologists like Malinowski and Mauss, in addition to these motives, still others come to the fore, for instance, giving based on feelings of mutual obligation. Lévi-Strauss argues that power and prestige may also be a driving force behind gift giving. In classical sociological and anthropological theories on social ties, generosity and self-interest are not necessarily opposites. In more modern theories, such as Hechter's, Mayhew's, or Etzioni's, this insight seems to have been lost. By combining sociological and anthropological theory, four main motives behind both exchange processes and solidarity come to the fore: affection, power, reciprocity, and self-interest or utility. These motives correspond to the models presented in Chapter 1. Yet another element connects the theories of solidarity and the gift, although it has received less attention in sociology than in anthropology: the ritual aspects inherent in the interaction processes that generate solidarity and reciprocal obligation.

The fact that solidarity may also have more negative and excluding aspects is addressed in Chapter 6. This chapter presents some empirical data derived from Dutch research on giving money to charity, giving time to volunteer work, and giving informal care to other people. In the Netherlands during the past decade the amount of money given each year to charity continues to rise. Since 1980 the portion of the Dutch population active in some form of volunteer work amounts to about one-third. Giving care offers the same pattern: since the 1970s those giving informal care to other people total about one-third. However, some inherent failures are connected to these positive manifestations of solidarity.

Introduction

For instance, research on gift giving shows that those who give many gifts (material as well as nonmaterial) also receive many gifts in return, but those who do not give much themselves – often because their social and material conditions do not allow them to do so – are also the poorest receivers. Informal giving mainly benefits those who already receive much; those who need it most receive the least. Solidarity may thus act as "a principle of exclusion." Solidarity appears to be selective in yet another way: those who offer care prefer their own family members and nearest relations over other persons in need of care. Those who do not have many family relations or near relatives are therefore at a disadvantage.

Traditionally the family has been considered one of the most important cornerstones of a harmonious and solidary society. Therefore family solidarity is the focus of Chapter 7. The combined demographic developments of the growing number of old and very old people and the decreasing number of young people have caused an increasing concern about family solidarity. Changed relationships between genders have contributed to this concern as well. Several theoretical dimensions of family solidarity are distinguished, and some empirical data on attitudes, feelings, and motives related to family solidarity are presented, as well as data on the amount of care provided to elderly family members. Family solidarity does not exist in a social void. The macrolevel of welfare state provisions is influencing the microlevel of informal care within the family, and vice versa, as some empirical findings have indicated. While intergenerational care is still provided on a large scale, particularly by women, the motives underlying it seem to be based on a kind of "prescribed altruism." Family solidarity is not necessarily or exclusively something positive, as is shown is Chapter 6. Both the provider and the recipient may experience it as a burden. Moreover, family solidarity cannot be isolated from the ambivalent nature of family ties in general.

Part III addresses some changes in contemporary solidarity and attempts to draw up the balance from the foregoing chapters. In Chapter 8 some broad societal changes supposedly having an impact on solidarity are briefly sketched: individualization, diversification, and globalization. Cultural critics often cherish a rather gloomy picture of the consequences of these developments for the mutual concern and social commitment of contemporary citizens. On the one hand, due to the individualization process social ties would have become more transitory and citizens would feel less committed to politics and societal concerns. A new personality type more self-reliant than ever before would have come into existence. On the other hand, the increased cultural and religious pluriformity and the growing multiculturalism in Western societies are assumed to have created much insecurity. Globalization is believed to create new opportunities while at the same time generating new social inequality. To counterbalance the views of these cultural critics, Chapter 8 presents also a more factual, empirically based overview of contemporary solidarity. Some traditional forms of solidarity have declined, others have been maintained, and also new manifestations of global and local solidarity have made their appearance. Civil solidarity as expressed in public behavior toward fellow citizens and the public space itself seems to have declined.

Chapter 9, finally, combines the insights derived from the previous chapters in a theoretical model with various dimensions of solidarity. One of these is the continuum of gift and sacrifice. The concept of sacrifice is hardly encountered in sociological theories on solidarity. Nevertheless, sacrifice is a characteristic aspect of some forms of solidarity. In anthropological theories gift and sacrifice are conceived as two manifestations of one underlying dimension. In the first case what is given is kept intact; in the second it is "sacrificed" (destroyed, burned, slaughtered, killed, and the like). In the theoretical model that is presented, the gift manifestation of the supposed solidarity dimension relies on mutual recognition, dependency, and reciprocity, whereas the sacrifice manifestation more often involves denial of personal autonomy and "otherness." Solidarity in small-scale social units is more likely to exhibit characteristics of the gift, whereas large-scale group solidarity is modeled more on sacrifice.

Introduction

With the help of this model it becomes possible to understand under which conditions solidarity will have positive or negative consequences for those involved. Finally, an attempt is made to characterize the essence of the transformation that solidarity has undergone in the course of the past century: from Durkheim's "organic" solidarity toward a solidarity that could be called "segmented," because the former mutual dependency of individuals and groups for the fulfillment of their needs is increasingly being replaced by autonomously operating segments that are showing solidarity on a voluntary and self-chosen basis.

Two final remarks are in order here, the first one about my use of concepts. It is obvious that the concept of solidarity harbors a multitude of dimensions and covers a range of phenomena of a very different nature: from giving to a beggar to organized worker solidarity, from offering help to your neighbor to walking in a silent march, from doing volunteer work to global networking. I deliberately refrain from attempts to give a full-blown definition of the concept that includes some aspects and leaves others out – which is what definitions amount to – because it renders every attempt contestable by necessity. I therefore decided to include those dimensions and manifestations of solidarity that are habitually accepted as such. The gift seems to be a less contested concept, although one might give some thought to what counts as a gift and why. This is done in Chapter 2. In the remainder of this book "gifts" refer to material as well as a nonmaterial gifts, like help or care.

Finally, my approach is analytical rather than normative. The conceptual framework developed in Chapter 9 is meant as a tool to understand why solidarity takes different forms and what these are, and why it may have different consequences for the well-being of the individuals and groups involved. It is not meant as a signpost for future solidarity. That is the domain of social and moral philosophy, which is outside the scope of the present work.

PART I

The Gift

Meanings and Motives

∾

ONE

The Social Meaning of Things

In any case all these things are always, and in every tribe, spiritual in origin and of a spiritual nature. . . . Each of these precious things . . . possesses . . . its individuality, its name, its qualities, its power.

(Marcel Mauss 1990 [1923]: 44)

Things are things, and people are people. Things are mute and inert; people speak and act with each other and are involved in the construction of shared meanings. This way of conceiving the distinction between people and things, common in Western society, is often contrasted with the views of non-Western societies, where things are supposed to possess a life of their own (Appadurai 1986). In some tribal societies described by Marcel Mauss in his classical *Essai sur le don* (1990 [1923]), things were considered as animated, or having a spirit (*hau*), communicating messages from the person originally in possession of the thing to its recipient. The spirit of the thing would not come to rest until it was returned to the place where its giver was born.

The opposition between Western and non-Western conceptions of things is clearly too simplistic. Many people will recognize that things may have a personal, often highly idiosyncratic meaning to them. For example, it is impossible for some people to throw anything away: for them the things with which they have surrounded themselves represent inalienable and highly cherished memories. We may also think of lovers who endow each other with little shells or stones found on the beach, symbolizing their affection. Small children suck at pieces of cloth, taking them to their bed and cherishing them as if they were animated. They get attached to their first teddy bears, sometimes developing such strong bonds that they still take them to their bed as grown-ups. Adults may worship some objects, such as the grail or religious items like icons, but destroy others – burning letters, smashing pottery, or throwing jewelry away. Both activities show that strong emotions may be connected to objects.

Clearly, things may embody different kinds of personal meaning, varying between attachment and aggression. In this chapter, I focus on things as depositories of social and cultural meaning. Things are a way to define who we are to ourselves and to others (Carrier 1995). Things convey symbolic messages, referring to the nature and (actual or desired) status of the relationship between human beings. Things are "tie signs," or signs of social bonds (Goffman 1971).

Social historians as well as social and economic anthropologists have pointed to the ways in which people inscribe meaning in the forms, uses, and trajectories of things. As Arjun Appadurai argues in *The Social Life of Things* (1986), it is not merely things but things-in-motion that illuminate their human and social context. Only the analysis of the trajectories of things enables us to interpret "the human transactions and calculations that enliven things" (1986: 5). In this view Appadurai is inspired by Georg Simmel's conception of (economic) value, as stated in his *Philosophy of Money* (1907). Value is never an inherent property of objects but is created in the process of exchange. An object gets value because one party's desire for it is fulfilled by the sacrifice of another object, which is desired by the other party. Economic life might, then, be considered as an "exchange of sacrifices." Rather than being a kind of by-product of the mutual valuation of objects, exchange engenders the parameters of utility and scarcity. The relationships and transactions in which they play a role create the value and identity of objects. This process not only generates economic value but also extends to symbolic value, embodied in the social and psychological meanings of objects.

The main question of this chapter is how things, in particular gifts, come to embody meaning within the context of human relationships. A specific focus on the meaning of things can clarify the differentiation in the nature of human relationships. This is important in view of the broader purpose of this book, which is to show that both motives to give and motives of solidary behavior depend on the nature of human relationships. Things-as-gifts, social relationships, community, and solidarity are inextricably tied to one another. First, I discuss different explanations of how things become invested with meaning, emerging from the sociological and anthropological literature. In those explanations, surprisingly, an account of the way meaning derives from the nature of social relations seems to be lacking. I present a model of the basic forms of human relations, derived from Alan Page Fiske's *Structures of Social Life* (1991). As we will see, his model may also be helpful to categorize the meanings of things. This model is then applied to some empirical data from a study on gift giving in the Netherlands (Komter and Schuyt 1993). Finally, I present a brief sketch of the complications that may occur when transactors do not share the same frame of mind with respect to each other and to the things that are transacted. When the meanings that things have for different people are not in harmony, things may have different, even conflicting, social lives.

Things and Social Relationships

There are many different kinds of things. In addition to goods that are transacted on the market, like utensils and food products, there are art objects, buildings, means of transport, but also plants, trees, and stones. Some of these things are suitable to give to other people as presents. A common way of thinking in the scientific literature of the 1970s and 1980s was to oppose commodities and gifts. Gifts were supposed to be personal and inalienable and to create social ties between humans, whereas commodities were thought to be alienable and to be exchanged between people who do not relate to each other outside the context of the exchange (Gregory 1982: Hyde 1983 [1979]). According to the logic that opposes gifts to commodities, people's relationships to things and to other people seem to fall in two broad categories that are regarded as mutually exclusive: either as impersonal, economic, or market relationships with strangers, or as personal gift relationships with intimates, friends, or relatives. Solidarity is, from this perspective, predominantly a matter of altruistic motives and is restricted to the second type of relationships. As we will see in Chapter 5, this is a far too limited and one-sided conception of solidarity.

The opposition between gifts and commodities is far less unequivocal than was assumed previously (Miller 1995a, 1995b, 1998; Carrier 1995; Davis 1996; Frow 1997). The distinction is mainly a matter of degree. Inalienability is not exclusively a gift characteristic, and commodities are not necessarily alienable objects. Goods may acquire cultural meaning in the course of time (Kopytoff 1986); think of utensils that take on artistic value later on. Commodities may become decommodified – a piece of jewelry once bought can gain personal significance and value – and non-commodities may become commodified, for instance, by selling one's blood or selling information (Corrigan 1997).

Many other parallels between gifts and commodities render an all-too-rigorous distinction dubious and put the concomitant distinction between two kinds of human relationship into question. In modern societies, the exchange of gifts as well as commodities is characterized by ritual, social, and symbolic aspects. Whereas this may be obvious for gift exchange (Komter 1996a, 1996b), the ritual elements in the consumption of goods and in market transactions should not be underplayed. One might think of modern consumption rituals, the ritual of trying to outbid each other at auctions, conspicuous consumption among the rich and powerful (Veblen 1934 [1899]), or customs of transacting business in "disguised settings" such as concert halls or restaurants, where other cultural and social aims – listening to music, having a meal together – are used as a cover for economic transactions. The things themselves do not possess some inherent meaning, but the trajectories in which they move render meaning to things. The gift economy and the market economy are interwoven in various ways, and gifts and commodities do not exclude one another. As Frow (1997: 124) says, "There is nothing inherent in objects that designates them as gifts; objects can almost always follow varying trajectories. Gifts are precisely not *objects* at all, but transactions and social relations."

Which economic, cultural, social, and psychological processes are involved in these transactions and how do these become embodied in things? Remarkably, many explanations focus on commodities and ignore the category of gifts. These, often Marxist explanations emphasize social structures, relations of production, and ruling ideas as the determinants of the meaning of things. Barthes (1973), for instance, argues that commodities act as a kind of "myths" supporting the existing ideology, thereby favoring those who are the most powerful in society. Similarly, Baudrillard (1988 [1970]) links goods and consumption to the overall economic order. Consumption is not tied to individuals but to the larger system of objects within that order. People's needs are not so much located in the individual person but rather in the practices of marketing and advertising. Manufacturers deliberately attempt to shape consumer behavior through advertising. The sector of production has "total dictatorship" over individual needs, according to Baudrillard. Whether the sector of production alone has, in fact, such overwhelming power is doubtful, but it is undeniable that advertising, marketing, and fashion are important instruments that render meaning to things.

Bourdieu's work (1984 [1979]) on the links between social class and the practices of consumption is another example of explaining the meaning of things by their role in sustaining existing social and economic power structures: people distinguish themselves from each other by adopting a certain life-style in which things or goods function as markers of their (aspired) status (e.g., paintings, books, objects of art). Acts of consumption, in his view, reproduce social difference because the consumption of some goods is considered a sign of distinction whereas consuming others signifies a lack of distinction. In a similar way McCracken (1990: 75) analyzes the meaning of goods in terms of the sociocultural categories of a certain society. Categories of class, gender, age, and occupation may be represented in goods: "[T]he order of goods is modelled on the order of culture." But the process also works the other way around: goods do not only embody cultural categories, but goods so charged "help make up the culturally constituted word. . . . In short, goods are both the creations and the creators of the culturally constituted world" (77).

The explanations presented so far refer to economic and social structures, advertising and marketing strategies, the ideology cementing existing power hierarchies, and sociocultural categories like class and gender. The emphasis on market goods not only undervalues the category of things transacted in nonmarket relationships, but at the same time implicitly reinforces the too-categorical distinction between gifts and commodities. No references to the specific trajectories of things between people are found in these explanations. This is striking considering that many different scholars have explicitly advocated this view (Appadurai 1986; Kopytoff 1986; Carrier 1995; Frow 1997). In the classical anthropology literature, which is mainly occupied with nonmonetary societies, the opposition between gifts and commodities is not yet visible. Here the meaning of gift exchange has been mainly conceived in functional terms: mutual gift giving serves to bring about social relationships, which, in their turn, are the cement of a common culture (Malinowski 1950 [1922]; Mauss 1990 [1923]). This view can be recognized in more recent contributions as well. For example, Titmuss (1970: 81–82), in his study of blood donation, describes the meaning of gift giving as follows: "The forms and functions of giving . . . may reflect, sustain, strengthen or loosen the cultural bonds of the group." In the same vein Cheal (1988: 40) describes the meaning of gift exchange as being a moral economy in which "the social significance of individuals is defined by their obligations to others, with whom they maintain continuing relationships. It is the extended reproduction of these relationships that lies at the heart of a gift economy, just as it is the extended reproduction of financial capital which lies at the heart of a market economy." Not fixed societal structures but the ever changing context of human relationship is taken as the point of departure to determine the meaning of gifts. It cannot be known in advance whether things are gifts or commodities. It depends on the nature of the social relationship within which things are exchanged.

Four Different Types of Social Relationship

Drawing on a broad range of classical and modern work in anthropology, sociology, and psychology, Alan Page Fiske (1991) develops an encompassing theory of the basic psychological motivations underlying social life. Human activities as diverse as arranging a marriage, performing religious rituals, making choices, judging what is morally right or wrong, or dealing with things can be ordered in four fundamental models: community sharing, authority ranking, equality matching, and market pricing. Integrating ethnographic, comparative, and experimental research with classical theory, Fiske demonstrates that people use different combinations and permutations of these models to shape their own identity, their motives, and their norms; to structure the way they relate to their environment; and to regulate their social roles and their participation in groups and institutions. These models also enable people to make sense of the way others behave toward them and to interpret their motives and intentions. The four relational models do not only orient people to other human beings in different ways; they also determine their relationships to nature – plants, animals – and to material objects, or things. "People can use each of the four fundamental models to organize transfers of material and nonmaterial goods and services and to provide obligatory or ideal standards for such transactions" (1991: 51).

According to Fiske *homo economicus* assumptions are predominant in many social science theories, from psychological learning theories, economically inspired game theories, and rational choice theories to equity and exchange theories. Against this monolithic tendency, he offers a multitude of examples from Western and non-Western cultures that demonstrate sharing, ranking, matching, and pricing behaviors. His hypothesis, supported by abundant cross-cultural, ethnographic illustrations, is that these behaviors are universal, "being the basis for social relations among all people in all cultures and the essential foundation for cross-cultural understanding and intercultural engagement" (1991: 25).

"Communal sharing" is conceived as a relationship of equivalence in which people attend to group membership, while the individuality and separate identity of persons are not very marked. Key words are identification, care, solidarity, and friendship. The experience of belonging to, and identification with, the collectivity is primordial. The terms of "kind," "kindness," and "kin," having a common Indo-European root, capture most of the features of communal sharing: "[I]t is a relationship based on duties and sentiments generating kindness and generosity among people conceived to be of the same kind, especially kin" (1991: 14). In community sharing things are mainly exchanged on the basis of feelings of connectedness to other people and out of a need to maintain the quality of human relationships. What one gives is not dependent on what one has received but springs from one's perception of other people's needs. In this model the things given will often be food, care, or services. Another category of giving within this model is not so much based on perceived need but on identification with other people. An important characteristic of things of this type is their sentimental value: who wore it or used it, to whom are you connected by means of these things? One may think of heirlooms, keepsakes, and any other objects, that symbolize precious memories. In all these examples, things are markers of "community."

In "authority ranking," the social relationship is characterized by asymmetry and inequality. People construe each other as differing in social importance or status. The highest-ranking people in a social relationship often have the prerogative of being accorded the initiative in social action, being the first who are allowed to make choices or to voice a preference. Those of high rank are more salient because they get more attention compared with their inferiors. Subordinates believe that their subordination is legitimate (although they may come to resist their predicament at some time). Purely coercive power in which people are dominated by force or threat is more often the exception than the rule in authority-ranking relationships. Within the authority-ranking model exchange is motivated by a (conscious or unconscious) desire to emphasize one's own status or power position. The perception of other people's relative power is an important factor in the selection of persons with whom one decides to transact. Power, fame, prestige, and merit are regarded as the most relevant criteria within social relationships. Transactions over valuable things are conducted with those high in the power hierarchy, whereas sops are good enough for those in lower positions. In contrast to the community model, the authority-ranking model also promotes showing and exposing valuable objects, in addition to exchanging items or giving such items to other people. Examples are conspicuous consumption, exhibition of prestige items, or symbols of rank and status. Clothes may function to symbolize status or group membership (think of children forcing their parents to buy exclusively branded articles like Nike shoes or Levi's jeans for them). For men cars are often symbols of status, power, virility, and sportsmanship. Women's jewelry seems to perform similar functions. In this model, things possessed (and exhibited) or exchanged are markers of superiority in power relations.

"Equality matching" refers to egalitarian relationships between peers. People have distinct identities but are in other respects each other's equals.

People share with each other, contribute to each other, and influence each other equally. In relationships of this type people have reciprocal exchange patterns, in which quid pro quo, or tit-for-tat, is the prevailing motivation. Rights, duties, or actions are conceived as balancing each other. People are interchangeable in the sense that it does not matter who gets or gives which share or who takes which turn, because everyone is equal and things come out even. The equality-matching model orients exchange in such a way that nobody benefits or loses disproportionally. Considerations in exchange are influenced neither by need nor by merit, status, or power. The items exchanged can often be aligned, weighted, or otherwise compared, enabling the participants to achieve equality by concrete operations of matching. Things exchanged in equality-matching relationships are tokens of balance.

In "market pricing" the relationship is dominated by values derived from the market. Rational choices and utility considerations determine how and when people will interact with others. People give and get in proportion to a common standard, reflecting market-pricing values like money, time, or utility. Market pricing and equality matching may be conflated or confused, when the profit-oriented element in quid pro quo reasoning gets too much emphasis. There is, however, a clear difference between the two: in market pricing, unlike commodities are exchanged in proportion to their market value, whereas in equality matching the same or equivalent things are exchanged. People's main preoccupation in exchange within the market-pricing model is: do I benefit from the transaction, do the costs involved outweigh the profits? People's relationships to others are instrumental, and often characterized by competition and struggle. One gives to those from whom one may expect some direct or future benefit. Things are tokens of utility or material (economic) value. It is important to bear in mind, says Fiske, that the distinction between the models is analytical in kind. Actual interpersonal relationships will, in most cases, be built out of a combination of these four basic psychological models. People use these models in the same way as they use grammatical rules, without necessarily being able to describe them reflectively, or even being aware of their existence. "My hypothesis is that these models are *fundamental*, in the sense that they are the lowest or most basic-level 'grammars' for social relations" (1991: 25).

Fiske emphasizes that the four models are not in any intrinsic way related to specific domains, as the work of some anthropologists suggests. Whereas both Malinowski and Sahlins presume that kinship distance is the primordial factor in determining the mode of exchange, Fiske argues that this is not necessarily the case: the same four patterns may emerge in any type of social relationship and in any domain, whether it be work, decision making, the meaning of time, social influence, the constitution of groups, the experience of self and identity, moral judgment, or dealing with things. Communal sharing may be the most typical within-group form of transaction, whereas exchanges between groups may often take the form of equality matching. Fiske's theory allows for other possibilities, although he does not reflect explicitly on these himself. For example, authority patterns and equality and market considerations may creep into interpersonal relationships. We might think here of sexually exploitative relationships, or of modern spouses or partners who, in the spirit of equality, share rights and duties in work and leisure, or who, like participants in market exchange, bargain meticulously about the division of household chores. Inversely, the community mode of relationship may penetrate the domain of the market and of institutional relationships, for example, when teachers or psychiatrists have love affairs with their pupils or patients, or when clients start having a personal relationship with prostitutes. That community is not necessarily restricted to the sphere of close kin and intimate friends is also exhibited in public charity behavior, in forms of empathic involvement with strangers in need, in situations in which people care disinterestedly for others as well as their own family or intimate friends, or when people offer hospitality to refugees.

A final word on Fiske's models may be in order. Within and across cultures, social relations are enormously intricate and varied; how can a general theory such as Fiske's encompass all this? Fiske takes great pains to demonstrate "how the set of four simple models can generate complex social relationships, roles, groups, institutions, and societies. People produce complex social relations by applying the models at a variety of levels (lower levels embedded – nested – within higher levels) and concatenating the models together in various combinations" (1991: 139). He offers theoretical as well as empirical answers to the question of how a few universal models can generate the great cultural diversity of social systems that can be seen around the world and throughout history. An attractive aspect of his theory is that it is not biased by a specifically Western view: the bulk of his illustrations are not from Western society but from ethnographic materials on the Moose of Burkina Faso.

In the next section I apply Fiske's models to research data from a study on gift giving in the Netherlands. My aim is to illuminate how a certain category of things, namely gifts, comes to be invested with meaning within the context of different types of human relationships.

The Four Basic Meanings of Gifts

In the study *Gift Giving in the Netherlands* (Komter and Schuyt 1993a) a questionnaire as well as in-depth interviews were used (the methods and design of the study are discussed more extensively in Chapter 2). In the interviews several of the basic meanings are revealed. For instance, gifts reflecting community are frequently mentioned. They symbolize the unique, highly valued, personal, and durable character of relationships. These gifts are not intended to evoke return gifts and seem mainly to be given out of sympathy, love, or the need to support another person. A single mother living on social security said: "I gave to my parents my little son's first shoe in silver as a Christmas present. It is a personal present in a double way, I think. Because I know that they have a small table with only silver objects on it, and on that table is also my own first shoe and my sister's first shoe silvered. So, I thought: I add my son's little shoe to that.

Because he is their first grandchild." A young woman mentions another example of such a precious personal gift: "I once asked my parents for my birthday to write in a booklet what had been important for them in their lives. I said that they were entirely free to decide what to write. And I asked them to return the booklet full, a year later for my birthday. And so they did. I valued this present enormously."

Within families money is sometimes given by (grand)parents to their grown-up children, just to offer some momentary relief or to make up for some more structural shortage of money. These gifts are unidirectional: no returns are expected, and even when the gift is given in the form of a loan, the expectation of return is vague and not specified in time. For example, a woman received € 150 from her parents: "They said: don't worry, we'll pay it for you. So I will return it at some time. If I happen to have some money, I may return it, but if I don't for some time to come, well, okay, then I don't pay it back."

Gifts reflecting community are not always material; also help offered disinterestedly, without any felt obligation, may illustrate community, as shown by a female respondent: "My daughter has to work many hours. Sometimes she has a day off, and then she has that enormous pile of clothes to be ironed. And then I say: come on, I will help you." Asked if she feels obligated to help, she says "No. If I would feel it as an obligation, then I wouldn't do it anymore. I simply do it because it's normal."

Authority, power, and dependency are very common aspects of relationships. However, people are not inclined to interpret gifts in these terms. Nevertheless, the interviews reflect those aspects in different ways. One way to emphasize one's superior position vis-à-vis another person and the rights and privileges that go with it is to give gifts that symbolize the subordinate position of the other person in a relationship, for example, by pointing to the role and tasks to be expected of this person: "When we were starting a family, I received some aprons from my husband. I wasn't happy with them at all. I was used to something more spiritual." Another female respondent told us: "My mother-in-law gave me some tea

towels for my birthday, as if she were saying: your place is in the kitchen."
These answers may be interpreted as reflecting "displaced meaning" in
McCracken's terms (1990: 117): goods that tell us not who we are but how
others wish we were.

Another illustration of authority and power is related to the phenomenon of the *potlatch*. The potlatch is a ceremony of competitive gift
giving and the collective destruction of wealth in order to acquire personal status and prestige. The ceremonial illustrates how abundant and
excessive gift giving puts the recipient in a position of almost impossible
indebtedness. Mauss (1990 [1923]) describes how the North American
Indians went so far as to destroy their wealth publicly instead of giving it
away – wasting one's riches as a sign of ultimate superiority and power.
Apart from the more caricatural examples in our own culture – the swimming pool filled with champagne, the bank manager lighting his cigar
with a thousand dollar note – excessive gift giving as a sign of power is
also a common practice in Western society. Our interviews revealed many
examples of gifts that were too many, too large, or too expensive, placing
the recipient in a position of undesired dependency. A male respondent
said: "I gave an expensive present to a woman from whom I expected
somewhat more than mere friendship in return, but she didn't feel like
that." Another example of gift giving causing dependency in the recipient is giving abundantly to a person who, for some reason, is not able
to reciprocate at some future time. A divorced woman living on social
security and being severely ill told us how difficult it was for her to accept
the lack of balance between gifts given and received by her: "I think that
it is more difficult to receive than to give. It is, uh, yes, it is sometimes a
bit of a burden. Then I think: gee, how can I ever make up for that, for
all the help that is given to me."

Equality is reflected in the expectations of reciprocity common to most
gift giving. Although the expectation of a return gift is very often not
consciously realized, the empirical pattern is that of reciprocal gift giving:
most gifts appear to be followed by a return gift at some point in time;

moreover, those who give many gifts receive many in return, and those who do not give much also receive the least (see Chapter 6 for more details). The underlying motivation is tit-for-tat – inviting others because they invited us, helping one's neighbor because he helped us, doing odd jobs for friends because you are expected to do so. A male respondent said: "I repaired the hallstand for her. She is old and, you know, a lamp was out of order. I repaired a plug, that sort of thing. And then the old woman said: here, take this; it belonged to my husband. It's Beethoven; he loved Beethoven, and now this complete Beethoven collection is yours, because you did all those jobs for me. . . . I appreciated that so much, that she gave her husband's favorite music to me."

Between parents and children reciprocity is often experienced in a special way: adult children often feel obliged to give their parents attention by visiting them or inviting them to dinner, because of what their parents have done for them when they were small children. A young man said: "I regularly visit my mother, every two weeks one afternoon. Then we talk together. She needs attention, she has just left the hospital. I find that okay: she has also given attention, extra attention to me when I needed it. Now she needs it. It is quite normal that I go to visit her." A Moroccan respondent emphasized the social and cultural necessity of the principle of reciprocity in a more general way: "Giving and receiving. In our society people have to give and receive. That's how it is. We ourselves receive as well as give. Otherwise life cannot continue, when one is not giving and not receiving."

Market pricing is shown, for example, in gifts that function as bribes. Although these gifts are more characteristic of the public sphere than the sphere of personal relationships, they are not totally absent there. Examples are gifts given to general practitioners by the pharmaceutical industry, gifts to political parties or politicians, or gifts meant as more or less subtle blackmail. But also in the interaction between friends, lovers, partners, and family members, instrumentality and calculation, an orientation toward personal benefit, may be reflected. A female respondent said: "My parents-in-law always give us very expensive gifts, as a kind of blackmail to visit them more often, by forcing us to be grateful." Although an element of authority is clearly present in this quotation – the giver placing the recipient in a dependent position by giving excessively – the market pricing aspect is revealed in the parents' attempt to "blackmail" their children.

Professional relationships are based on a market model: services are offered in exchange for money. When an employer gives a standard Christmas packet to his employees, this is not merely an expression of his gratitude for performed services but also an attempt to strengthen the employees' commitment to the company. The employer's motives to give this gift remain within the confines of the market model. However, professional relationships may take on other connotations, for instance, those deriving from the community model: university professors giving more than normal attention to their students, barristers receiving more than financial compensation for their services. A quotation from a barrister illustrates the difference between economic and personal recompense: "Yes, giving a present has a different connotation, because people have to pay a bill as well, so if they give something extra, then it has often a personal tinge. It has a different content. The economic value doesn't interest me at all, but it *was* special."

Conflicting Social Lives of Things

The potential use of Fiske's typology may be further illustrated by attempting to explain the conflicts that may occur in the social life of things. In interpersonal relationships people's interpretations and valuations of things may not correspond with each other. Things may lead conflicting social lives, in that the meanings people attach to them may not harmonize. Differences between people's attitudes toward things may be the source of disagreeable misunderstandings and serious disputes. Conflicts may arise between people when things represent a different value to them or embody different sets of expectations and different courses of action that need to be undertaken.

For example, things experienced by one party as markers of community may be considered by another party as mainly interesting because of their market value. Examples may be found in the often fierce and long-lasting family disputes about legacies. We may think of an heirloom cherished by one inheritor because of the inalienable and unique memories it embodies, whereas another relative emphasizes its monetary value and wants to sell it on the market. In fact, what the surviving relatives are quarreling about is the symbolic value of the object as it is experienced by each of them. The inheritor who succeeds in imposing his will to sell the object is in fact denying and even annihilating the special and personal value the object had for the other relative.

Many other examples present themselves. A thing given out of love or community sharing may be received with indifference and, in the long run, be reciprocated with a return gift in the spirit of equality matching. Humiliating gifts may degrade the recipient and destroy his or her expectations of community or equality. Gifts given to mark the authority of the giver over the recipient, for example, gifts consciously or unconsciously meant to make the recipient somehow dependent upon the giver – a money gift to someone who is less wealthy, or a learned book to someone with only rudimentary education – may be misjudged as signs of love and personal interest: community in Fiske's terms. Even merely market-inspired attempts to manipulate or bribe someone, or to induce him or her to do a return favor by means of giving a gift, may be misinterpreted as a token of community: a sign of personal attention and love.

Things: Markers as Well as Marks of Relationship

The transaction of things may be regarded, in the terms of Appadurai (1986: 21), as a "tournaments of value": a complex social process in which the value of things is determined by developing "a broad set of agreements concerning what is desirable, what a reasonable 'exchange of sacrifices' comprises, and who is permitted to exercise what kind of effective demand in what circumstances" (1986: 57). These value tournaments not only determine the economic value of things but also form the context in which other symbolic and social meanings of things are developed. The (economic) scarcity of things is only one of the relevant dimensions within exchange relationships. Things may come to embody the values of community, be used to emphasize authority, underscore equality between exchange partners, or express economic or market values. These values are not inherent in the things. Neither is it merely the form or ceremony of the transaction that renders meaning to a thing. As Carrier states, it is, instead, "the relationship that exists between the transactors and the relationship between them and what is transacted" (1995: 19).

Things, then, far from being static, inert, and mute, may be compared with other more current vehicles of meaning such as words. Like words, things are part of an informational system, the meaning of which is created within the context of social interaction and mutual communication between people. Due to the various emotions they invoke in people, and to the contests of value to which these emotions are exposed, things come to embody differential meaning. Like words, things play a dynamic and active role in creating, maintaining, disturbing, or destroying human relationships (think of returning a wedding ring or throwing away or destroying gifts received).

As Douglas and Isherwood have observed in their anthropological theory of the consumption of goods, things work as markers or classifiers: "Treat the goods then as markers, the visible bit of the iceberg, which is the whole social process. Goods are used for marking in the sense of classifying categories" (1979: 74). But the coin has another side as well: goods are both the creators and the creations of the culturally constituted world. Similarly, one might argue that relationships not only get meaning by means of the trajectory of things, but, inversely, that things derive their meaning from their place and role within relationships. Things are markers as well as marks of relationship.

∞

In this chapter we have sketched the global framework in which the social meaning of things comes into being. The meaning of things was found to correspond to four models of human relationships. Focusing our analysis on gifts as one important category of things, the four broad meaning categories were confirmed by some empirical data on gift exchange. These four meaning categories return in many of the following chapters, as they represent general motivations that are pertinent not only to gift exchange but also to solidarity.

A very important notion for the rest of this book is Simmel's idea of the "exchange of sacrifices." In every exchange act something is sacrificed, and the value of what is exchanged is determined by the participants' beliefs of what represents a fair and reasonable exchange. The concept of sacrifice will prove to be a crucial one for the gift as well as for solidarity. Not only things but also people may be sacrificed in exchange. Human beings may sacrifice their own self by giving away abundantly, whether in material or nonmaterial form. Also other people may be sacrificed by means of a gift – think of the fatal poisoned cup Roman emperors used to offer. Similarly, in solidarity self as well as others may be sacrificed. These ideas are further elaborated in Chapter 9.

It is now time to explore some other patterns and meanings of giving in more detail. Social and psychological patterns of giving and receiving are the focus of Chapter 2. In Chapter 3 the role of feelings of gratitude within the chain of reciprocity in gift giving is discussed, while Chapter 4 examines the gendered meanings of gift giving.

∞

TWO

Patterns of Giving and Receiving

Gifts may reflect unfriendliness in at least two final ways. First, the gold watch presented at retirement is normally more representative of a feeling of good riddance than of recognition for achievement; it is indeed a gilded "pink slip." Lastly, psychoanalytic theories of symbolism suggest that death wishes may be expressed in such gift objects as electric trains, satin blankets, ships, and other vehicles which take "long journeys." Inasmuch as such theories are valid, the popularity of electric trains as Christmas gifts has enormous implications.

(Barry Schwartz 1996 [1967]: 75)

When giving something to another person, our intentions are often not entirely unselfish. We expect that our gift will be reciprocated by a suitable return gift; otherwise we have the feeling that there is something wrong with our relationship to the recipient of our gift. Anthropologists like Malinowski, Mauss, and Lévi-Strauss investigated the impact of moral obligation for the creation of social bonds and a shared culture in non-Western societies and showed that mutual gift giving is an important mechanism behind social cohesion and solidarity. The focus of this chapter is on some fundamental social patterns underlying gift giving in Western societies and on some of the main social-psychological aspects of giving.

From within the discipline of psychology not much empirical research on gift giving has been done, although recently this tendency seems to shift (Otnes and Beltramini 1996). As concerns theory, the main sources of inspiration are still found in the classical anthropological and sociological literature on gift exchange. Although the theme of the gift has great psychological significance – it is related to human identity and to a multitude of positive as well as negative motives, emotions, and feelings – psychologists have largely ignored the subject. Exceptions include Barry Schwartz (1967), who has studied gift giving from the perspective of "bad gifts," or gifts that have unfriendly intentions. Offensive or embarrassing gifts may cause psychological harm and seriously threaten social ties.

Gifts tell something about the identity of both the giver and the receiver. Gifts mirror ourselves, but they reflect the identity of the recipient as well because the gift symbolizes the way we perceive the recipient. In the act of gift giving the giver pays respect to the person of the recipient and affirms his personal identity. To the recipient the gift symbolizes that he or she is recognized as a person having a special value to the giver. Feelings of moral obligation and gratitude on the part of the recipient will be the result, making him offer a return gift.

After a discussion of some empirical research results on giving and receiving in some Western societies, this chapter explores the main psychological functions of gift giving. Then the psychological motives that may underlie gift giving are connected to the four basic meanings of gifts as distinguished in Chapter 1. If we want to understand the meaning of the gift for the disruption as well as the formation of social ties, we should also pay attention to the less positive side of gift giving. Because social ties and feelings of solidarity can be undermined as well as created by gift giving, the chapter considers those offensive and embarrassing gifts reported by the respondents of our study on gift giving in the Netherlands.

The Gift: Empirical Research

Although there is almost no psychological research into gift giving, the related disciplines of sociology and social psychology offer some interesting research results. In general the principle of reciprocity is assumed to be the rule in gift giving (Gouldner 1973a), but this principle does not apply to certain types of gifts, such as organ or blood donation. If at all, in these cases reciprocity is experienced in a very indirect and abstract way. Reciprocity is, as it were, delayed: if, at some future time, we might come to need blood or organs ourselves, we hope that other people will be as willing to give as we were.

In one of the first empirical studies into gift giving in Western society the sociologist Titmuss (1970) compared blood donation in Britain with that in the United States. Almost all British donors appeared to donate blood voluntarily, while at that time (toward the end of the 1960s) blood donation in the United States occurred mainly on a commercial basis. The corollary of this difference was that American donors had predominantly a low education, were unemployed in most cases, and belonged to ethnic minorities. In contrast, the British donors were a better representation of the population at large. In the United States receiving blood proved to be related to social class: the higher the social class, the more blood one received. So, the poorer part of the population gave their blood to their more wealthy compatriots. In view of the higher mortality and morbidity of the lower social strata, one would have expected the reverse. Apparently, class-related factors like better access to and benefit from health care of the higher social classes play a role here. Finally, Titmuss's study shows that the risk of contaminated blood (at the time mainly hepatitis B, as the AIDS era had not yet started) was substantially higher in the American, commercial way of organizing blood donation than in the British system.

A second empirical study into gift giving has been conducted in America by the sociologist Caplow (1982a, 1982b). He interviewed 110 adults in "Middletown" on Christmas gifts. One of his main findings was a powerful gender effect: women proved to be very active as givers in terms of thinking about what to give and then buying and wrapping gifts. Alone or together with their husbands they gave 84% of all gifts, while receiving 61%. Men gave only 16%. Of all gifts 4% went from men to men, against 17% of gifts from women to women. Men gave the more expensive gifts, but there was no significant difference in the financial value of the gifts received by men and women. There was also an effect of age: the majority of gifts goes to the younger generation. In his theoretical interpretation Caplow stresses that we are particularly inclined to give to others when we are not yet completely convinced of their good intentions toward us.

Caplow (1984) also examined the unwritten rules regulating gift giving. For instance, there are rules concerning the emotional value of gifts within different types of relationships; the marriage relationship counts as most valued, followed by parent-child relationships, and so forth. In intimate relationships a different type of gift is given than in more businesslike relationships: an envelope containing money is not appropriate for one's partner, whereas money gifts are acceptable when given to colleagues. Particular occasions ask for particular categories of gifts: at funerals you are supposed to bring flowers rather than cake or champagne. The rules surrounding gift giving are complex. Most often things run smoothly, but sometimes we make mistakes, for instance, giving a wrong-sized garment. As Caplow observes, "Women are particularly resentful of oversized items that seem to say the giver perceives them as 'fat'" (Caplow 1984: 1314; see also Shurmer 1971).

The Canadian sociologist Cheal (1986, 1988) has studied the practice and meanings of gift giving and criticizes the dominant theoretical approach of gift giving within the sociological discipline: exchange theory (Emerson 1902 [1844]; Blau 1964). Exchange theorists assume that people give to other people exclusively because they expect a direct or indirect recompense. Cheal, however, conceives of gifts as a symbolic means to establish or maintain social ties. Gift giving is not merely the exchange of more or less useful objects but also, and predominantly, a process of "emotion management," to use Arlie Hochschild's term (1979), concerned with the emotional aspects of social relationships. Characteristic of a gift is its redundancy, according to Cheal. Giving a gift is not strictly "necessary." Unlike the political economy, where the redistribution of necessary resources and profit making are the ruling principles, the gift economy is not ruled by the iron law of necessity. The unexpected gift in particular illustrates its redundancy. Upon receiving such a gift, we are inclined to respond with: "Oh, you shouldn't have!" indicating that the gift was not strictly necessary. In his own empirical research Cheal combined qualitative interviews among 80 adults with a large-scale survey among 573 adults in the Canadian city of Winnipeg in which he focused on Christmas and wedding gifts. Gift giving again appeared highly gendered. Inspired by Goffman, Cheal writes how men, by means of their gifts, may reinforce existing power differences: "In particular, he described 'the courtesy system' through which men convey the belief that women are precious, ornamental and fragile. Rituals of this sort have a place in the social construction of female dependence" (Cheal 1987: 152).

In Winnipeg, as in "Middletown," women appeared to do the largest part of the "gift work." Cheal attributes this finding to women's traditional responsibilities for maintaining social contacts. This would mean that women's larger share in gift giving is explained by the traditional gender roles and the gendered division of labor and care outside and within the home. In Chapter 4, this explanation, together with a number of alternative explanations for women's generosity in gift giving, is reviewed in more detail. Cheal's research data show that women were not only the greatest givers but the largest group of recipients as well. More than half of all gifts recorded in this research went to women; it is likely, says Cheal, that many of the gifts with joint male and female receivers were also given to women. Between spouses there often existed an asymmetric pattern: men gave more expensive gifts than women did, even when both partners earned comparable incomes. According to Cheal, this may be interpreted as a form of symbolic control of men over women.

In our own research into gift giving in the Netherlands we examined giving as well as receiving (Komter and Schuyt 1993a). Before I review the methodology of this research, some remarks about the definition of a "gift" are in order. What exactly is to be considered as a gift? Using the respondents' own definition of what they experience as gifts is apparently a good approach. However, this would imply another type of research than we had in mind. Because we were mainly interested in the sociological patterns of gift giving and in the psychological motives underlying these patterns, and not primarily in the subjective definitions of "gifts" as opposed to "nongifts," we distinguished several giving objects or giving activities, material as well as nonmaterial: presents, monetary gifts, hospitality (inviting people to dinner or letting them stay in one's house). Our idea was that, in spite of obvious differences between them, practices such as ritual or spontaneous gift giving, offering help or care, or hospitality to other persons have one very essential aspect in common: all these gifts are imbued by the subjective experience of being given out of free will and are not being dictated by any economic rule such as fair exchange or barter. Although this experience may in many instances boil down to an illusion because in the long run most acts of gift exchange do seem to fit within a cycle of reciprocal exchange (Bourdieu 1990 [1980]), its subjective validity is not undermined by this fact: most people do honestly believe that they are acting freely and voluntarily when giving gifts to other persons. Moreover, although many gifts in fact can take on an economic aspect (care or help can be bought and sold, presents can be stripped of any personal meaning and become merely a matter of value, such as book tokens, coupons, and money gifts), many people, at least when they have some material resources and enough time at their disposal, seem to prefer the personalized form of gift giving – giving as a means to express personal feelings toward other people – above the economized form. A possible definition of gift giving, then, goes as follows. Although gift giving in most cases objectively conforms to the principle of reciprocity, subjectively it is felt to be an essentially noneconomic, spontaneous, and altruistic activity, meant to communicate personal feelings instead of being an exchange transaction.

Our main and very simple research question was: who gives what to whom, and why? A series of questions, derived from this main question, was posed as to the several kinds of gifts we had distinguished – for example, Did you give or receive any gift during the last month? To or from whom did you give or receive this gift? What was the occasion? How did you feel about giving or receiving this gift? A questionnaire with mostly precoded and some open questions that was sent to 3,000 households from all over the country was returned by 513 respondents, aged between twenty and seventy (a response rate of 17%). The sample was drawn at random from the Register of Addresses of the Dutch Postal and Telegraph Service. On most relevant criteria (gender, age, education, religion, and marital status) our sample appeared to be a reasonable reflection of the general Dutch population. However, no pretensions of complete representativeness can be upheld because of the rather low response rate, which is not uncommon with this research procedure. In addition to the questionnaire, 99 respondents from Amsterdam or its near surroundings were interviewed extensively. The same set of questions as in the questionnaire was posed, but more probing was done on subjective feelings surrounding gift giving and on psychological motives to give. Here too, as many women as men participated, but there was a slight overrepresentation of the higher educational levels and incomes. Interviews were recorded and transcribed verbatim. Research data were analyzed quantitatively as well as qualitatively.

In the questionnaire and interview, the first question was, Have you given or received any . . . during . . .? For presents and dinners the period meant here was the preceding month, in our case September 1992; for money gifts, hospitality, and care or help, the period comprised the preceding nine months. More than three-quarters of our respondents appeared to have given some of these gifts, and more than half of the respondents report having received one or more of these gifts from others (see Table 2.1).

TABLE 2.1. Have You Given or Received
Any Gift during the Preceding Month
(presents and dinner) or the Preceding
Nine Months (money, stay, care)?
(%; N = 513)

	Given	Received
Presents	86	64
Money	84	53
Dinner	70	58
Stay	65	41
Care/help	65	55

Source: Komter and Schuyt (1993b).

A strong relationship appeared to exist between giving and receiving. Those who gave most, were also the greatest recipients. Apparently, doing well has its reward. Not only in Malinowski's and Mauss's non-Western cultures but also in our own society the principle of reciprocity is the underlying rule of gift giving. It is, however, striking that everybody feels they give more than they receive. If we assume that this result reflects a factual truth and not some perceptual bias, the most plausible explanation is that an important category of gift recipients, children, is not included in the sample. But other interpretations are possible too, for example, the role of memory. Perhaps people have a greater consciousness of what they have given themselves than of what they have received from others. Furthermore, there might be a perceptional bias: because one wants to leave a generous impression of oneself to the interviewer, one is inclined to exaggerate one's own liberality. Or, inversely, one's discontent about what one has received from others leads to underestimating it. Perhaps people make unconscious or conscious comparisons between their own resources and those of others, which might explain their experience of discontent. Yet another interpretation might be that some forms of giving are not recognized as such by their recipients; for example, some types

TABLE 2.2. Have You Given or Received
Presents, according to Gender,
Education, and Age? (%; N = 513)

	Given	Received
Gender		
Male	84	55
Female	90	75
Education		
Low	80	50
Middle	87	67
High	91	71
Age		
20–34	88	70
35–49	90	65
50–	81	58

Source: Komter and Schuyt (1993b).

of received care may be overlooked, because they are so "normal." A
final explanation might be what Pahl has called "the general concern of
people not to appear too dependent on others" (1984: 250). His finding
that people claim to do more for others than they receive in return seems
to correspond with our results concerning the experienced imbalance
between giving and receiving.

Certain categories of respondents appeared to be greater givers than
others, as is shown in Table 2.2. This finding applies to all kinds of
gifts, material as well as nonmaterial (for more details, see Komter
1996b). Women, the more highly educated, and younger people give
more presents; the same categories give also more hospitality and more
care and help. How can these patterns be explained? As we have seen,
a possible explanation for women's greater gift giving is that thinking about, buying, wrapping, and giving gifts traditionally belong to
women's tasks and responsibilities within the home (Cheal 1988). Also,
women are more likely than men to develop sets of reciprocal responsibilities with kin (Finch and Mason 1993). As said before, a more

elaborate theoretical discussion of women's liberality is postponed to Chapter 4.

The greater gift giving of the more highly educated might not only relate to their greater financial resources but also to their often less traditional and less stabilized relational patterns, compared with less educated people. Contrary to what is often thought, and to what has been found in earlier research (Bott 1957), the social networks of the more highly educated people and those higher in the social hierarchy are often more numerous and more extensive compared with the networks of the lesser educated (Young and Willmott 1973; Douglas and Isherwood 1979). Within these extended networks, gift exchange probably serves to stabilize and sustain social relationships. The same reasoning may explain why younger people give more than elderly people: because patterns of relationships are not yet stabilized, any change brings new flows of material and nonmaterial gifts.

Psychological Functions of Giving

The first psychological function of the gift is to create a moral tie between giver and recipient. Gifts make people feel morally bound to one another because of the mutual expectations and obligations to return the gift that arise as a consequence. Gifts can perform this moral function because they are "tie signs," in Goffman's terms. Almost anything can serve as a gift, from expensive objects bought in fancy shops to a freshly cut flower or a small shell found on the beach. Gifts are endlessly variable resources that help us to express our feelings toward other people and, particularly, to inform them about the nature of the bond we have in mind.

A second psychological function of gift giving relates to the disclosure, affirmation, or denial of identities of giver as well as recipient. As Schwartz (1967) has argued, gifts are disclosing identities in a double way. On the one hand, they reveal how we perceive the recipient, and how we evaluate his or her taste, preferences, and needs. On the other hand, our gifts disclose something of our own identity, our own feelings toward the recipient: our own being, personal taste, cultural values, and financial resources. The gift is, as it were, a "looking-glass-self," to use Charles Cooley's concept: acting like a mirror, the gift reflects ourselves in the picture we have formed of the recipient.

Both personal and social identities have their impact on the mutual expectations that arise through gift giving. For instance, social identities like age and gender often determine the type of gift that is given. Many gifts are gendered, with women's gifts including perfume, lingerie, or jewelry, and men's gifts including socks, neckties, or cuff links. Different types of gifts for adults and children exist. In many gifts, however, the mark of personal identity is more important than that of social identity. The closer the relationship, the less one has to resort to the supra-individual characteristics of the recipient, such as gender and age. By disclosing part of our personal identity in our gift, we express our special feelings for the recipient. We are somehow what we give. In giving something to another person, we give something of ourselves, our own being (Mauss 1990 [1923]). Thanks to the enormous variety of possible gifts, we are able to choose exactly that gift we think will cause the recipient the greatest possible pleasure. A gift thus demonstrates our recognition, acceptance, and estimation of the recipient. In our gift, particularly chosen for this person, we show not only our investment in terms of money and time but also, and more important, our emotional involvement with this particular person, including his or her idiosyncrasies and shortcomings. This gift confirms the identity and self-esteem of the recipient.

A respondent from our research told us, for instance, what it meant to her to be invited for dinner: "I feel this is so important. And I think it's the same for other people. It's a way of showing, eh, mutual respect. That you are interested in what other people feel and think." Another respondent, who is a vegetarian, said: "Some people have tried so hard to be creative in their cooking a vegetarian meal. I appreciate that so much. Apparently they like me, then." To indicate the feelings of self-esteem or self-respect caused by receiving a gift, some authors have used the concept of "honor" (Mauss 1990 [1923]; Bourdieu 1990 [1980]). A respondent told us that she always felt somewhat "honored" when she receives something from another person, because it shows that this person has spent some of his time thinking about her and actually obtaining something she would really like as a present. On being a giver herself, she told us: "I always hope that they will feel honored as well, not because it's *me*, but because somebody has thought about you a lot. It also expresses something like: you are worth it, that I do this for you."

A gift, then, can be regarded as recognition of the other as a person and as a sign of honor, respect, and appreciation. But, as becomes apparent in the next two sections, the reverse is also possible: through gift giving we may hurt another person by offending his or her personal identity and self-esteem. The psychological consequences of such a gift may be far-reaching and even result in the discontinuation of the relationship. The gift is a psychological vehicle that may threaten or undermine identities. Why are we doing this? What motives are underlying our gifts?

Motives to Give

It is not so much the content of the gift but its spirit that counts. Not the object itself, but the motives and feelings of the giver determine its impact on the recipient. The value of a gift is predominantly measured according to the personal investment that has been put into it, and not so much according to its monetary costs. Self-made presents to which much personal attention, effort, and time are spent figure among the most valued gifts. One cherishes the gift of a piece of jewelry that belonged to an ancestor, not so much because of its economic value but because of the memory it embodies. The small shell from the beach that lovers give to one another represents minimum economic but maximum symbolic value. In that particular shell all the love of the world resides. The material aspect of a gift is subordinate to the motives of the giver.

What psychological motivations are involved in gift giving? In what follows, an attempt is made to categorize motives. Where possible, illustrations from the Dutch study on gift giving are used. These illustrations are drawn mainly from the field of care and help because these motives were most clearly crystallized and more easily expressed than was the case with the other giving activities (psychological motives to give are often largely unconscious).

Positive Feeling

A first and most common category of motives expresses friendship, love, gratitude, respect, loyalty, or solidarity. These gifts have as their main purpose to communicate our positive feelings to the recipient. Some of the motives reported by our respondents are strongly other-directed and altruistic: one wants to contribute to another person's well-being without thinking about a return service; one helps or cares because one feels a general moral obligation to do so. The most important moral criterion in people's considerations concerning their gift giving is related to need: one gives because the other needs it, without expecting any return in the first place. One example involves a female respondent who helps her demented mother with her finances: "Yes, you should do that as a daughter, I think. You don't receive in return so much anymore, but that is not important." And: "I am a human being, so I have to help a fellow human. That's how it is."

However, even such gifts may (consciously or unconsciously) have a strategic aim. For instance, gifts may express our desire to forgive, to repair some wrong in the past, to ease our conscience, to flatter, to attract attention, or to maintain our presence in someone's life. Giving to charity is another example of benefiting another person while at the same time relieving our own conscience. The latter example clearly shows that contributing to another person's welfare may serve one's own self-interest at the same time.

Insecurity

A second and again very common class of motives relates to insecurity – for instance, about the status of the relationship. By means of giving a gift one may hope to reduce the uncertainty. As Caplow argues, the majority of gifts are given in order to ascertain and fortify relationships that are deemed important but have not yet been stabilized. In the same vein, religious offerings may be regarded as attempts to reduce insecurity. By means of offerings, humans express their gratitude toward the deity, thereby reducing their insecurity about the hereafter and increasing their hopes to obtain grace. Related to the insecurity motive but of a different intensity and background is the motive of anxiety. We may give because we are afraid to lose a cherished relationship, or as an attempt to ward off a potential danger. Or we can give to show a potential or real enemy that we have good intentions and want no harm.

Power and Prestige

Gifts may also be inspired by a need for power and prestige or by considerations related to reputation and fame (Bailey 1971). By means of giving a gift we are putting ourselves in a morally superior position; we may cause the recipient to feel indebted, sometimes to such an extent that we even claim some rights on the basis of our gift giving. In many non-Western cultures gift giving was inspired by rivalry: givers try to surpass one another in generosity, thereby asserting their power. The more one gives, the more prestige, power, and honor one is accredited with. The most extreme example of this is the earlier mentioned potlatch (see Chapter 1). Offering exquisite banquets, giving expensive bouquets of flowers, or organizing fancy parties – these are all modern examples of potlatch where the recipient is, as it were, stunned by the gift. Giving an overly generous gift that cannot be reciprocated properly is humiliating. Giving gifts may serve to dominate and to make others dependent upon our benevolence and our willingness to share valuables and resources with them.

Reciprocity, Equality

A fourth large category of motives is related to psychological expectations of reciprocity and equality. The underlying idea is that favors have to be reciprocated with equivalent value: I will give you something, because I expect that you will return my gift in due time or when necessary (for instance, in the case of help). Most of the reported motives are of this mixed type: there is a propensity to give, but before doing so an inner calculus is made about the respective participants' position on the "debt-balance" (Schwartz 1967). Feelings of being morally obliged to return a gift and not purely altruistic motives are the main psychological impetus to reciprocal giving. A deeply felt need to render a service to another person is lacking here; equality is the moral criterion: "I looked after their children by way of compensation: my brother-in-law helped me with my doctoral thesis. More of a compensation than a real joy, yes." Another respondent went doing odd jobs for friends, although he did not like it in the least: "It is stupid work. I did my own home not so long ago, and I still am heartily sick of it. But those are the things friends are expected to do for each other, mutually."

Self-Interest

A fifth class of motives is based on implicit or explicit self-interest, either taking the shape of promoting one's own interests or by disadvantaging or harming the recipient. A range of possibilities is present here: gifts that serve to flatter, propitiate, corrupt, blackmail, or bribe. The entire world of sponsoring but also segments of political and professional life feed on this idea. Many gifts in the sphere of public life hardly cover up the self-interest that motivated them – for instance, the pharmaceutical industry offering golf weekends to physicians and their partners, concluded by a light scientific program on the advantages of certain pharmaceutical products. Particularly, the larger business gifts are close to a bribe. Money gifts may be used for all kinds of dubitable aims: as hush or redemption money, or as a means to obtain certain societal or political gains. Although gift giving has earlier been defined as a voluntary and spontaneous act, some gifts are not allowed to be given freely, as is shown by the fact that gifts to political parties have been forbidden by the law in many countries.

Our respondents sometimes make a sharp calculus about the debt balance between give and take: does the other person not profit too much from my gift giving? Does what I receive from others measure up to what I gave myself? Personal costs and gains are the main motives here. Giving, in this case, is based on a kind of market model, in which personal costs and benefits form the dominant considerations. One male respondent who felt that his neighbors had asked him too often to perform all kinds of small jobs for them, said: "At one moment I felt that I was taken advantage of; well, then it is the end, for me. It's different when it is coming from both sides, but here, there is only one party who does all the giving. Well, then I am finished with it." And another one says: "It is nice playing open-handed Gerald always, but there has to be *some* return at some time." Or: "Others help me too, yes. Otherwise I would not do it, I think. I am not going to make a fool of myself."

Hostility, Hate, Contempt

Finally, in addition to, or sometimes even combined with, the motive of self-interest, motives related to hostility, hate, or contempt may inspire our gift giving. Gift giving as an intentional act of unfriendliness is perhaps a less usual way of looking at the phenomenon but is not uncommon. The extent of the hostility may vary from relatively harmless practical joke gifts, like the exploding cigar or the jack-in-the-box, to gifts motivated by really deep-seated feelings of anger, hate, or disdain.

We may give a gift to someone who has affronted us or treated us badly in order to let this person sense how ignominious his action has been. Aggression can be the underlying motive of a meager gift given to somebody whom we used to bestow with abundant gifts in the past. Anna Freud's "altruistic surrender," abundant giving to a person of whom one is intensely jealous and whom one deeply hates for that reason, is another example (A. Freud 1986 [1936]).

Fiske's Four Models and the Motives to Give

The four models of human relationships outlined in Chapter 1 can clearly be recognized in the psychological motives described here. However, although the models correspond to some of the motives, the models do not cover the motives entirely. The motives reveal more of people's motivations to give than the models do. This comes as no surprise because Fiske's models are based mainly on sociological and anthropological material. The statements of our respondents, quoted in Chapter 1 as illustrations of the models, make clear that there are four ways in which people may relate to gifts and, through these gifts, to other people: community, authority, equality, and market. The first category of motives mentioned earlier, the positive affect, seems akin to the type of feelings involved in community, the model that has disinterested concern and commitment to other people – often family and loved ones – at its core. However, the strategic aspects that may go with gifts apparently given out of "pure love" – the want for attention, the wish to make up for some wrong or to soothe one's conscience – show that community may be too superficial a way to describe what is going on in a social relationship based on sympathy. Moreover, motives like insecurity or anxiety may very well underlie gifts given within the mode of community: lovers giving abundantly to one another, thereby trying to diminish their insecurity about the status of their relationship, or children giving loyally to their parents because they are afraid to lose their affection.

Motives arising from a need for power and prestige are in accordance with the relational model of authority. But here, as well, the motives of insecurity and anxiety may accompany the power motive and complicate its meaning. As Adorno's famous research on the authoritarian personality makes clear, insecurity and anxiety are often at the roots of authoritarian ways of behaving (Adorno 1950). Expensive or abundant gifts given with the aim to acquire a superior position over other people or to make them dependent upon us may, at a deeper level, reflect the fundamental insecurity about the impact and efficacy of the respective resources of giver and recipient and, thereby, about the status of the relationship.

A very common type of motive in gifts is the self-evident giving "because it's only normal," the tit-for-tat reflected in the relational model of equality. When a friend invites us to dinner, we bring flowers or wine; she does the same, when dining with us, just because it is the normal thing to do. The reported motives based on self-interest are corresponding to the relational mode of the market. Self-interest may go together with hostility and aggression, but this need not be the case. Gifts given by the pharmaceutical industry to the physicians are motivated by self-interest but are not expressing hostility. Hostility is an additional category of offensive motives that may occur in any of the four relational modes, thereby complicating their impact. Just as disappointed or frustrated love (Fiske's community) is susceptible to turning into aggression, so can relations normally characterized by authority or equality become perverted by anger or vengeance.

In many fairy tales malevolent gifts play a prominent role, for instance, Snow White's poisoned apple. In the Introduction we have seen that the German and Dutch word *Gift*, meaning poison, has its etymological roots in the word "gift." Some gifts are literally given with the intention to sacrifice somebody's life; think of the legendary poisoned cup. In the following section examples from our own research (Komter and Schuyt 1993a) show how, behind the cheerfully colored wrapping of the gift, intentions of the giver may be hidden which are not in the least congruent with the recipient's frame of mind toward the giver.

Offensive and Embarrassing Gifts

Although the role of conscious intention in giving an offensive gift is limited, gifts are often experienced as such by their recipients. Even if it were one's explicit intention to give an offensive gift, it is probably difficult to admit that to an interviewer. Here we are faced with a fundamental difficulty that underlies any attempt to measure motives of this kind. It is extremely difficult, if not impossible, to capture the motives underlying gift giving because the act of gift giving is in most cases barely reflected upon. It is therefore not surprising that only a small minority of our respondents – 8% – report that they have ever given an offensive gift; 10% have received an offensive gift at some time. When using a more friendly term like being "embarrassed" by a gift, the pattern changes: 21% of the respondents have given an embarrassing gift to another person, and 31% say they had felt embarrassed by a received gift. On the basis of our respondents' stories about offending and embarrassing gifts, we developed four categories of "bad gifts."

First, some gifts are simply not appropriate: "An acquaintance gave me after-shave, although I have been wearing a beard for twenty-five years"; "wine but I don't drink alcohol"; "a couple of geese, although we already have so many animals"; "jeans that were too small"; "a ridiculously expensive vase from an amorous colleague." Second, there are thoughtless gifts, or gifts that are too easy, bought in haste, or already in the giver's possession and then passed on: "a nasty little floral emblem for my farewell after having been the president and vice-president of the company for twenty-five years"; "two ceramic cats – supermarket rubbish – while I am a ceramic sculptor myself"; "a 1992 calendar, received in August 1992." Third, some gifts are pedagogical in the sense that they point to another person's weaknesses, criticize him or her, or communicate a form of uncalled-for advice. For example, one respondent reports that she has given a scale to someone else as a Christmas present "in order to let him weigh things out"; other pedagogical gifts are antiperspirants or shampoo or soap, "as if I smell bad"; or advice books about "how to bring up your dog" or about how to cope with alcohol addiction. Finally, there is the category of trash and monstrosities: castoffs such as "a used teapot"; "a bag with second hand clothes, which was ready for the trash can"; and monstrosities like "a fishbone plate," "a screaming-green floorlamp from my grandmother," "a small net to cover plates, which was so cheap it fell in pieces immediately."

The many ways in which one may offend or embarrass other people with one's gifts are presumably reflected in the deeper meaning of the adage that you "should not look a gift horse in the mouth. Gift giving is inherently risky, exactly because of its psychological function of disclosing identities. Gift giving is a game with an uncertain outcome. One does not bargain about gifts, and that is precisely what distinguishes gift exchange from economic exchange.

The Debt Balance: Source of Relational Risks

One important effect of the gift is that it serves to recognize the value of the recipient as a person. But gift giving is at the same time a very risky activity, precisely because identity is so crucially involved. One potential risk is that the recipient does not share the feelings we want to express in our gift. Our well-intentioned gift may cause disappointment, disapproval, irritation, or embarrassment in the recipient. With our gift we may have forced ourselves too much upon the recipient. We sometimes project our own feelings onto the other person: a gift out of compassion toward another person may, in the end, reflect our own self-pity; a great love for us supposedly felt by another person may be reduced to our own feelings of love for him or her. We may misjudge the taste or the needs of the recipient, or the nature of our relationship to the other person, causing him or her to reject the gift. This is an extremely painful event, as the rejection of the gift may not only reflect that we had a wrong image of the recipient but also, and more seriously, imply a rejection of our own personal identity and being by the recipient.

Gifts reflect, confirm, disturb, or injure identities. The motives used in this interactional process range from love and sympathy, to insecurity and anxiety, to power and prestige, to self-interest and overt hostility. Gifts may be conciliatory as well as estranging and distancing; they may be saving as well as sacrificing lives. This enormous psychological potential of the gift has been largely ignored so far. In order to prevent gifts from becoming perverted, it is extremely important to keep the subtle balance between giver and recipient intact. Giver and recipient find themselves involved in a debt balance with respect to one another. This balance should neither be in complete equilibrium nor disintegrate into disequilibrium. Giver and receiver should be in an alternatively asymmetrical position on this balance, each party properly reciprocating the gift received, thereby preserving the equilibrium. The extent of asymmetry can only be held in control by the specific type of feelings usually evoked by a gift: gratitude. Not being able to feel proper gratitude, exaggerating or underplaying one's own gratitude, not acknowledging gratitude in the recipient, under- or overestimating his or her gratitude: all of these imperfections can severely disturb the debt balance and generate great relational risks.

∝

Three insights can be derived from the current chapter that are important in view of the theoretical model that is developed in the course of this book and specified in Chapter 9. A first building stone for our argument is the reciprocity principle for which empirical support has been presented in this chapter. The reciprocity of giving and receiving is a crucial element in our model of solidarity. A second aspect concerns the insight that gifts reflect identities. Gift exchange is based on the mutual recognition by givers and recipients of each others' identity. Without that recognition it would be impossible to render meaning to gifts themselves; for gifts reveal both the identity of the giver and his perception of the recipient's identity. Finally, the commonly accepted idea that gifts have merely positive consequences for social relationships is disproved in this chapter. Negative aspects and consequences are also connected to solidarity, in the sense that some people are excluded from the community whereas others are included, although sometimes at the cost of their own autonomy.

∞

THREE

The Anatomy of Gratitude

Gratitude and resentment, therefore, are the sentiments which most immediately and directly prompt to reward and to punish. To us, therefore, he must appear to deserve reward, who appears to be the proper and approved object of gratitude; and he to deserve punishment, who appears to be that of resentment.

(Adam Smith 2002 [1759]: 81)

In our commonsense thinking about gratitude, we are inclined to think of it as a warm and nice feeling directed toward someone who has been benevolent to us. The definitions of gratitude given in dictionaries confirm this perspective. Although I think that this view contains an important element of truth, it disregards a more fundamental meaning of gratitude. Beneath these warm feelings resides an imperative force, a force that compels us to return the benefit we have received. Gratitude has a clearly specified action tendency connected to it, as Adam Smith had already noticed and as is also stipulated by contemporary emotion theorists (Lazarus and Lazarus 1994). This duty to return led the social psychologist Barry Schwartz (1967) to speak of the "gratitude imperative." Why aren't we allowed to look a gift horse in the mouth? Because that would be a sign of ingratitude and of indifference toward the giver, and that is simply disastrous. In Japan the recipient of a gift is not allowed to unwrap it in the presence of the giver. To Western eyes this may seem an exotic habit, but on closer inspection it contains a very important message about gratitude: by keeping the gift wrapped, the recipient's possible disappointment about the gift and its giver – showing itself in a lack of gratitude – remains hidden. Perhaps this is the Japanese version of our gift horse.

Why is a lack of gratitude felt as something to be avoided by all means? Because gift exchange and the attendant feelings of gratitude serve to confirm and maintain social ties. Gratitude is part of the chain of reciprocity and, as such, it has "survival value": it is sustaining a cycle of gift and countergift and is thereby essential in creating social cohesion and community. Gratitude is the oil that keeps the engine of the human "service economy" going, to use Frans de Waal's term (1996).

But gratitude is not merely a moral coercion; it is also a moral virtue. Gratitude as a virtue is an important aspect of character: the capacity to experience as well as express feelings of being thankful. The fact that somebody may be seen as a grateful person indicates that gratitude is a personality asset, a talent or even a gift that permeates all the social relationships in which this person is involved. Lacking this virtue results in ingratitude, which seems to be an enduring personality characteristic as well. People who are regarded as ungrateful incur the risk of becoming isolated and estranged because of their inability to contribute to the essential symbolic nourishment on which human relationships are fed – that is, the mutual exchange of gifts connecting people by the bonds of gratitude.

The linguistic meanings of the word "grateful" are revealing. In English as well as Dutch, "grateful" has a wider range of meanings than the literal one of being grateful to somebody for having received something. The first meaning becomes clear if we speak of a "grateful shade" where the word is synonymous with salutary or pleasant. In "grateful soil" the word means fertile, able to produce abundance without much outside help. In Dutch we speak of a "grateful task" or a "grateful subject," indicating that the task or subject promises its own reward without much extra effort (gratitude itself seems to be this kind of subject!).

I refrain here from trying to give a full-blown definition of gratitude, because definitions of such multilayered and complex phenomena are bound to be inadequate. What I can do, however, is sketch the contours of an "anatomy of gratitude," in an effort to delineate some of its most prominent aspects and meanings. I approach the subject from various angles, starting with the very thing that is given away. Anthropological perspectives on the "spirit of the gift" wanting to be returned to the original donor are the focus here. Next I consider the recipient of the gift and analyze gratitude from a psychological point of view, as a personality characteristic. How do people develop the capacity to be grateful and express gratitude toward others? Then, from a sociological point of view, I focus on the mutual relationship between the recipient and the giver and the social and cultural impact of gratitude. Reciprocity appears to be the underlying principle behind gift exchange, with the connected feelings of gratitude functioning as the moral cement of human society and culture as such. Without gratitude there would be no social continuity as it fosters and maintains the network of social ties in which we are embedded.

The Spirit of the Gift

Let us first examine some of the most seminal insights on gifts and grati-tude formulated by anthropologists. According to them, one of the main characteristics of gifts is that they should be given and reciprocated. A gift that cannot "move" loses its gift properties. A very clear example is the Kula, the ceremonial exchange of gifts by the inhabitants of the Trobriand Islands near New Guinea. Malinowski, who lived among them during the First World War, describes this ritual in detail in *Argonauts of the Western Pacific* (1950 [1922]). The Kula is a form of exchange on the part of the communities inhabiting a wide ring of islands, which form a closed circuit. Along this route, articles of two kinds constantly travel in opposite directions. Long necklaces of red shell move in a clockwise direction, whereas bracelets of white shell move in a counterclockwise direction. After some time, these articles meet articles of the other class on their way and are exchanged for them. It takes between two and ten years for each article in the Kula to make a full round of the islands. This practice shows that it is not the articles that count but the exchange itself, the principle of give-and-take, as Malinowski terms it. The important thing is that the Kula gifts are kept in motion. If a man keeps a gift too long, he develops a bad reputation. Somebody who owns something is expected to share it, to pass it on. Among the Trobriand Islanders, to possess is to give, as Malinowski says.

Another example of a gift cycle can be found in Mauss (1990 [1923]). In his essay on the gift he describes the habits and traditions of the Maori, the native tribes in New Zealand. The Maori have a word, *hau*, which means spirit, in particular the spirit of the gift. Returning from the forest where they have killed birds, the hunters of these tribes give a part of their game to the priests, who cook the birds at a sacred fire. After they have eaten some of them, the priests have an offering ceremony in which they return the *hau*, in the form of a part of the birds, to the forest where it is supposed to produce a new abundance of birds to be killed by the hunters again. As occurs in the Kula, there is a cycle of gift giving: the forest gives its richness to the hunters, the hunters give it to the priests, and the priests return it to the forest. The ceremony performed by the priests is called "nourishing *hau*," feeding the spirit, a literal form of feedback. The spirit of the gift is only kept alive by returning it to where it comes from. By placing the gift back in the forest, the priests treat the birds as a gift of nature.

The key idea of Maori law is that the thing given or received is not inactive. After a thing has been abandoned by the giver, it still possesses something of him, *hau*. Through *hau*, the giver has a hold over the recipient because, as Mauss writes, "it is the *hau* that wishes to return to its birthplace, to the sanctuary of the forest and the clan, and to the owner." The spirit of the gift remains attached to the chain of beneficiaries until they give back from their own property, "their goods, or from their labour or trading, by way of feasts, festivals and presents, the equivalent or something of even greater value." The legal tie in Maori law, a tie occurring through things, is "one between souls, because the thing itself possesses a soul, is of the soul. Hence it follows that to make a gift of something to someone is to make a present of some part of oneself" (1990 [1923]: 12). Therefore, the recipient of the gift "must give back to another person what is really part and parcel of his nature and substance, because to accept something from somebody is to accept some part of his spiritual essence, of his soul. To retain that thing would be dangerous and mortal." The reason for this is that things do not only come from persons morally but also physically and spiritually. Gifts exert a magical or religious hold over people. The thing given is invested with life and "seeks to return to . . . its 'place of origin'" (13).

Several scholars of authority have criticized Mauss for his spiritual interpretation of the *hau*. Firth (1929), for example, prefers secular to spiritual explanations. According to him the fear of punishment or social sanctions is the real reason to fulfill one's obligation to return a gift. These sanctions can include a threat to the continuity of economic relations or to the maintenance of prestige and power. Another anthropologist, Sahlins (1972), offers an alternative explanation, which is secular as well. Returning to the original text of the Maori legend, he discovered an interesting aspect that Mauss had neglected in his rendering of the story. The participation of a third party in the cycle of gift exchange is crucial to Sahlins's conception of *hau*: for a gift to bring increase, it is necessary that a third party causes this increase. In the Maori legend, after having received the birds taken by the hunters, the priests offer some of them to the Mauri – a sacred stone acting as a shrine – which can then cause the birds to abound. According to Sahlins, the term "profit" would have been a better translation of *hau* than Mauss's "spirit." Sahlins conceives of *hau* as the "increase power" of the goods of the forest. The ceremonial offering of birds by the priests restores the fertility of the forest. In Sahlins's words, "the *hau* of a good is its yield, just as the *hau* of a forest is its productiveness" (1972: 160).

More recently, the French anthropologist Maurice Godelier (1999) reevaluates the various interpretations of *hau*. Godelier interprets the game the hunters give to the priests as an "offering of thanksgiving in the hope that the forest and the priests will continue acting on behalf of the hunters" (1999: 52). According to him, the essential idea in *hau* is that the original donor retains his rights over the object he has given regardless of the number of times it changes hands. Here he is paying tribute to the work of the late Annette Weiner (1992), who analyzed the Kula ceremonials from the perspective of "keeping-while-giving." She stated that certain categories of objects, in particular sacred objects, are given and kept at the same time because their ownership is inalienable in the end. Objects may circulate, and every person who receives them becomes a donor in turn. But only the original donor has the ultimate rights over the object because his ownership is inalienable; the other donors merely enjoy alienable and temporary rights of possession and use, which they transfer when they pass on the object. Following Godelier's view, it is not so much the spirit or the soul of the gift that makes it want to return to its original owner, or its profit or yield, but rather the owner's inalienable rights over the object, which are known, felt, and respected by the other donors. Godelier makes an interesting shift here from explaining the return of gifts on the grounds of properties of the object itself to attributing the cause to characteristics of the recipient, namely his original rights: he replaces the animistic and spiritual interpretation with a psychological and personal one.

However interesting Godelier's interpretation in terms of the first donor's rights may be, the spiritual explanation cannot so easily be dismissed. In many other tribal communities, there are examples of things that are thought to possess a spirit, to be animated or alive, to have a will of their own, to wish to return to where they originally come from. An animistic way of experiencing things often originates in situations where natural fertility and growth are felt to be important. Lewis Hyde (1983 [1979]) describes a practice among American Indian tribes who depend on the ocean for their primary sustenance, especially the salmon that annually enter their rivers. The salmon are believed to dwell in a huge lodge beneath the sea and to have a human form when they are at home. Only once a year they change their bodies into fish bodies, swim to the mouths of the rivers, and sacrifice themselves to their land brothers as food for the winter. The first salmon in the rivers is welcomed with an elaborate ceremony. The fish is caught, placed on an altar, and laid out before the group with its head pointing inland to encourage the rest of the salmon to continue swimming upstream. According to Hyde,

the first fish was treated as if it were a high-ranking chief making a visit from a neighbouring tribe. The priest sprinkled its body with eagle down or red ochre and made a formal speech of welcome, mentioning . . . how much the tribe had hoped the run would continue and be bountiful. The celebrants then sang the songs that welcome an honoured guest. After the ceremony the priest gave everyone present a piece of the fish to eat. Finally . . . the bones of the first salmon were returned to the sea. The belief was that salmon bones placed back into the water would reassemble once they had washed out to sea; the fish would then revive, return to its home, and revert to its human form. . . . If they were not, the salmon would be offended and might not return the following year with their gift of winter food. (1983 [1979]: 26–27)

This beautiful Indian story, demonstrating the idea that gifts of nature can only bear fruit if people show them gratitude in a proper way, clearly illustrates the action tendency of gratitude. The view that natural wealth should be treated as a gift is as old as the Old Testament, where the first fruits of the earth are perceived as belonging to God. The fertility of the earth is a gift from God, and in order to continue it, its fruits should be returned to him (Hyde 1983 [1979]). Perhaps this religious origin of gratitude also has an ecological aspect. Throughout history, people have had some sense that it is wrong to usurp the wealth offered by nature. Traditionally it has been a common practice among European farmers to let their fields rest after they had intensively cultivated them for some time. It is difficult to separate the religious awe felt by humans for the abundance of the earth from their feeling that they should not exhaust its resources.

Hyde describes another interesting category of gifts where gratitude can be seen at work, namely gifts given at funerals. Gratitude apparently not only binds the living to nature and to one another; it also connects the living to the dead. Gifts given at someone's death are part of a general class of "threshold gifts" that mark the passage from one state into another. By means of these gifts, the transformation from one identity to another is facilitated. Often some attributes pertaining to the life of the deceased (human or animal) are inserted into the coffin: pharaohs are buried with their most valuable treasures and jewelry, and children are accompanied by their most cherished toys on their journey to another state. Many people believe that corpses should be buried with gifts intended to help the soul on its journey. If the dead are not properly laid to rest, they will walk ceaselessly on earth, according to some folk beliefs. Gifts not only help transform the identity of the once living being into the now dead one; they also express our gratitude to the deceased, to the fact that we knew them and enjoyed the privilege of being in their company for a certain period of time.

Hyde speaks of gratitude as a "labour undertaken by the soul" to effect the transformation after a gift is received. "Between the time a gift comes to us and the time we pass it along, we suffer gratitude. . . . Passing the gift along is the act of gratitude that finishes the labour" (1983 [1979]: 47). In this final act, the true acceptance of the original gift is accomplished. The spirit of the gift has been kept intact by giving ourselves away: our ties with people who are or were dear to us have been renewed and strengthened.

How people react to natural abundance and how they create and main-tain mutual bonds by exchanging gifts can be interpreted in terms of the concept of gratitude. Malinowski's principle of give-and-take seems to be based on an underlying feeling of indebtedness to the giver, which we are now inclined to call gratitude. Gifts returned to nature because nature "expects" us to do so and gifts "wanting to return" to where the original giver lives both seem to indicate an inner feeling of obligation to the outside world, which is projected onto that world. That sense of obligation can only be resolved by means of an act of gratitude. Also the story about the "spirit of the gift" can be regarded as a metaphor of gratitude. The difference with our modern conception is that gratitude is not thought of as an internal feeling or emotion but as an external force that compels the recipient to reciprocate. Perhaps this conception of gratitude derives its compelling force exactly from the fact that it is externalized and objectified: acting in the spirit of gratitude is felt as a generally endorsed obligation that you cannot afford to shirk on the penalty of social disapproval and exclusion.

The Recipient of the Gift

From a psychological point of view gratitude may be considered a virtue, a personality characteristic, or asset. It is something one has to learn, and some people are better equipped to learn it than others. Learning to say thank you, to share, and to return is an important part in the education of children. What are the preconditions for developing a capacity to be grateful? In her essay "Envy and gratitude" (1987b [1957]), Melanie Klein considers gratitude from a psychoanalytic point of view. She holds that envy is the most powerful factor in disturbing feelings of love and gratitude at their root, because it originates in the earliest relation of a child to its mother. This relationship has a fundamental importance for the individual's whole further emotional life, according to Klein. The quality of the mother's earliest breast contact with the child and, more symbolically, of her capacity to represent to the child a "good object" with which it can identify is of great importance for laying the foundations for hope, trust, and belief in goodness. Any deprivation in this respect, not only the breast's literal failure to provide enough milk but also – and more important – the mother's withholding of emotional nourishment, may cause the child to develop a serious emotional impairment in the form of hate, envy, jealousy, or greed.

The most significant consequence of this emotional impairment is that the child is deprived of the opportunity to experience enjoyment as a result of being satisfied by the good object. Envy tends to become such a persistent characteristic because it spoils the capacity for enjoyment; enjoyment gives rise to gratitude, and only gratitude can mitigate destructive impulses like envy and greed. Only children who have been able to develop a deep-rooted relationship with a good maternal object can build up a strong and permanent capacity for love and gratitude, which can withstand temporary states of envy and hatred. In Melanie Klein's words, "One major derivative of the capacity for love is the feeling of gratitude. Gratitude is essential in building up the relation to the good object and underlies also the appreciation of goodness in others and in oneself. Gratitude is rooted in the emotions and attitudes that arise in the earliest stage of infancy, when for the baby the mother is the one and only object" (1987 [1957]: 187).

Just as Freud describes the infant's bliss in being suckled as the prototype of sexual gratification, Klein considers these experiences as constitutive for all later happiness. The full gratification of the maternal breast brings about the experience of having received a unique gift from the loved object, a gift that the child wants to keep. This first gift is the basis of gratitude. The gratitude of being satisfied enables a child to accept and assimilate to the loved primal object, not only as a source of food but also as a whole person. This is the first sign of basic trust in other people. The more regular the gratification and the more fully it is accepted, the more often the child will experience enjoyment, gratitude, and the wish to return pleasure in its wake. This recurrent experience plays an important role in the capacity to return goodness. Here we can see how gratitude and generosity become connected. Only inner wealth makes one able to share gifts with others. As Klein says, "if this gratitude is deeply felt it includes the wish to return goodness received and is thus the basis of generosity. There is always a close connection between being able to accept and to give, and both are part of the relation to the good object" (1987 [1963]: 310).

The idea of a relation between the absence of shortages in motherly dedication and the capacity to enjoy the first gifts a child receives from its caretaker (whether it be milk, warmth, or closeness) sounds highly probable. Also the hypothesis that one should first develop a capacity to enjoy the good things one receives from others before being able to experience gratitude seems reasonable enough. Finally, the connection between gratitude and generosity, the idea that the capacity to receive and be grateful fosters the desire to return goodness seems theoretically plausible. The principle of reciprocity that is demonstrated in so many of the anthropologists' accounts apparently applies at the level of the earliest interactions between mother and child as well. A lack of basic love and care – the first gift – leads to a failing capacity to enjoy, which in turn impairs the capacity to be grateful and to return the gift. As in all gift relationships, the bond is only kept intact if gifts are returned properly. Both the mother and the child may fail in this respect. In that case the negative side of the principle of reciprocity may come to apply. The less the mother is capable of giving the best of her being to the child, the less responsive and grateful the child will become. An ever more disturbed relationship may develop if the child does not give in return, causing the mother to become less responsive as well. Just as the gift of gratitude paves the way for new gifts to be given, a lack of gratitude evokes a diminishing propensity in others to give return gifts.

It is clear that there are substantial individual differences in the capacity to experience and express gratitude. Some people are much more able to express genuine gratitude and be generous without compromise than others. Gratitude is a personal virtue that is neither self-evident nor equally distributed among all human beings. Not only do individuals differ in their capacity to be grateful; there are also culturally varying expressions of gratitude, as the example of Japan mentioned at the beginning of this chapter made clear. Nevertheless there seem to be culture-independent functions of gratitude.

Gratitude, Reciprocity, and Culture

Gratitude: The Moral Memory of Mankind

A sociological view on gratitude stresses the interpersonal relationships and social interactions in which gratitude takes shape. Gratitude is always embedded in a relationship between two parties. The capacity to be grateful and generous develops within the context of a social relationship. The primary function of gift giving – creating social ties – is clearly demonstrated in the interaction between mother and child: the bond is only kept alive and intact if there is some degree of positive reciprocity. Gratitude plays a crucial role in establishing and maintaining social relations. At the beginning of the twentieth century, the sociologist Georg Simmel wrote his beautiful essay "Faithfulness and gratitude," one of the few texts to address the subject of gratitude directly. He called gratitude "the moral memory of mankind" (1950 [1908]: 388). By mutual giving, people become tied to each other by a web of feelings of gratitude. Gratitude is the motive that moves us to give in return and thus creates the reciprocity of service and counterservice. Although it has psychological feelings at its base, its main function is social, according to Simmel. Gratitude functions within the chain of reciprocity. Gift exchange and the concomitant feelings of gratitude are at the basis of a system of mutual obligations among people and, as such, function as the moral cement of human society and culture. Simmel also refers to the role of gratitude in fostering the continuity of social life. Gratitude connects people with what has gone on before and gives them the continuity of interactional life. He conducts a mental experiment by imagining what would happen if every grateful action based on benefits received in the past were suddenly eliminated: society would definitely break apart. Gratitude not only creates and smooths interpersonal relationships; it also fulfills important cohesive functions for society and culture as such.

The social nature of the principle of reciprocity is very clearly illustrated in the fascinating animal research data collected by Frans de Waal and his co-workers (1996). After having offered ample illustrations of chimpanzees sharing and exchanging food, de Waal asks the crucial question why. In his experiments, he observed chimpanzees when they see a caretaker arrive with bundles of blackberry, sweet gum, beech, and tulip branches. Characteristically, a general pandemonium ensues: wild excitement, hooting, embracing, kissing, and friendly body contact, which he calls a "celebration." De Waal considers it a sign that indicates the transition to a mode of interaction characterized by friendliness and reciprocity. Celebration eliminates social tensions and thus creates a setting for a relaxed sharing of the food. Perhaps the chimpanzees' basic feeling of delight preceding the sharing of food can be compared with the joy of children receiving the good object from their mother, as described by Melanie Klein. Perhaps celebration and joy are preconditions of the harmonious being together in which the first acts of reciprocity can take place. De Waal's results clearly demonstrate that celebration is followed by a pattern of reciprocal giving and receiving: those who share with others will also receive from others, and those who are poor givers will be poor recipients as well. Apparently, animals have the mental capacity to keep track of what they have given and received and apply this capacity whenever it is appropriate (de Waal 1996).

A sociological pattern of reciprocity is exactly what we found in our study on gift giving in the Netherlands (Komter and Schuyt 1993). Although certain categories of respondents appeared to be greater givers than others – women, younger people, better-educated people – reciprocity was the rule among all the categories in about the same degree. The principle of reciprocity not only applied to material but also to non-material gifts, as we have seen in chapter 2 (Table 2.1).

Gratitude, Power, Dependence

Thus far, I have spoken about gratitude only as a positive emotion and a social force bringing about community and cohesion. However, gratitude is not always the positive and unproblematic phenomenon we would like it to be but may be complicated by issues of power and dependence. For instance, the principle of reciprocity can be disturbed if returns are not equivalent. One party may not have enough resources to meet the other's expectations of what counts as proper returns. Power may be involved in reciprocity, causing asymmetry, with one party feeling it should give, or being actually obliged to give, much more than the other. In such cases, gratitude looks different than in situations dominated by more or less symmetrical reciprocity.

The sociologist Alvin Gouldner (1973a) was the first to elaborate upon the role of power in situations of asymmetrical reciprocity. The respective levels of the resources of giver and recipient should be taken into account, as well as the needs of the recipient and the freedom the giver has either to give or not. Giving may be compelled by other people or by strong normative expectations to do so, thus restricting the spontaneity and voluntariness of the gift giving. This probably affects the way gratitude is experienced. Unfortunately Gouldner, like most of his sociological and anthropological colleagues, does not elaborate upon that particular subject.

As is often the case with really fundamental issues, literature offers some interesting insights that are notoriously absent in the social science field. The Russian writer and poet Marina Tsvetajeva, who wrote most of her work just after the Russian Revolution in 1917, has a very uncommon but enlightening view on the vicissitudes of gratitude. She deeply mistrusted the Bolshevik rulers and their oppressive political tactics. This distrust was reciprocal. The Bolshevik regarded Tsvetajeva as a hostile element and obstructed publication of her work, necessitating her to live with her two small children in one icy room at her parents' house. Poverty and hunger made her dependent on alms offered to her by friends and acquaintances from time to time. In this type of situation, gratitude looks quite different from what we are used to. What feelings toward the giver does a poor person have on receiving a loaf of bread, and what kind of expectations does the giver have? In analyzing this example, taken literally from her own life, Tsvetajeva claims that the actors here are not a real giver and a real recipient, each with their own person reflected in their actions, but merely a giving hand and a receiving stomach. When a stomach receives bread, this has nothing to do with the personal being of either the giver or the recipient. It is merely two pieces of flesh that are involved in the act of exchange, and it would be absurd for one piece of flesh to demand gratitude from the other. Gratitude, in that case, would degenerate into paid love, prostitution, and be an outright offense to the giver as well as the recipient.

As Tsvetajeva says, only souls can be grateful, "but only because of other souls. Thank you for your existence. Everything else is offense" (2000: 201). Ultimately only silent gratitude, gratitude not expressed in words or acts, is acceptable because the mere expression of gratitude already implies some reproach or humiliation for the giver: he has something the recipient does not have, a painful confrontation between having and not-having. The best solution is to give, to receive, and then rapidly to forget about it, so as to preclude any feelings of gratitude at all: to give and withdraw, to receive and withdraw, without any consequences. In such an unequal power relationship, the moral obligation to express gratitude is derogatory and an obstacle to the development of lasting ties.

In gift exchange, a subtle balance of dependence and independence is involved, causing power and control to be deeply ingrained. Schwartz called this the balance of debt, as we saw in Chapter 2. Depending on the personal biography and specific psychological makeup, people react differently to this balance of debt. Some have great difficulty receiving help or material goods from others, because they cannot deal with feelings of gratitude or being indebted to another person. The balance of debt may be disturbed in several ways. One means to exercise power is to keep another person indebted by way of overreciprocation. Another offense is to return a gift too quickly. Giving immediately in return can be interpreted as a sign of ingratitude. As Seneca stated, "a person who wants to repay a gift too quickly with a gift in return is an unwilling debtor and an ungrateful person" (quoted in Gouldner 1973a: 258, n. 46). A certain period between the gift and the return gift is also needed, because the resources to be able to return the gift properly have to be found and mobilized. The reason why, according to Schwartz, the balance of debt should never be brought into complete equilibrium connects to gratitude: "The continuing balance of debt – now in favour of one member, now in favour of the other – insures that the relationship between the two continues, for gratitude will always constitute a part of the bond linking them" (1967: 8).

Not only a disequilibrium on the debt balance but also rivalry may disturb the "normal" development of feelings of gratitude, as is demonstrated in the potlatch. Gift giving in this practice should not be confused with acting on the grounds of a moral obligation to return gifts. What is seemingly an act of gratitude is ultimately one of power and greed.

In the preceding sections, gratitude appears as a personal asset as well as a moral virtue: a capacity one has to learn. Moreover, gratitude has been analyzed as the moral basis of reciprocity. By acting as a moral obligation to give in return, gratitude not only serves to reinforce bonds at the level of social relationships, but is also a means for establishing social cohesion and creating a shared culture. It is important, at this point, to emphasize that indebtedness is not in any way contrary to gratitude but rather is its moral core.

Gratitude Dissected

Five conclusions can be drawn at this point. First, a theory on gratitude should integrate its psychological, moral, social, and cultural dimensions.

Like "the gift" itself, gratitude proves to be a truly interdisciplinary subject. Views from anthropology, psychology, and sociology each highlight different aspects and add different emphases. Second, gratitude is part of a chain of reciprocity and has "survival value": it is sustaining the reciprocity of service and counterservice, and it is universal. Third, gratitude is a response to a voluntary gift but is itself "imperative": not showing gratitude when it is appropriate leads to social disapproval and exclusion. Fourth, gratitude derives its social importance and effectiveness from the moral obligation implied in it. Fifth, gratitude can be a positive as well as a negative force – for instance, in a context of dependency and power inequality.

Where do the various reflections on gratitude presented in this chapter bring us? Is it possible to formulate a tentative theory that integrates the various insights and pays justice to the enormous richness of the theme of gratitude? All of the views discussed have a strong and inescapable force in common, one that compels recipients to give in return, and it is this mysterious force that lies at the heart of gratitude. The force is alternatively thought to reside in the given object, in nature, in the person of the recipient, or in the social relationship existing between the giver and the recipient. A theory on gratitude should offer us some understanding of the specific nature of this force. Let us, therefore, scrutinize more closely the various layers that are embedded in the views outlined here.

The first layer of gratitude is a spiritual, religious, or magical one. Related to this view is an ecological level, since in any case, the origin of the force asking for restoration of the equilibrium is located outside human beings, in nature or in spiritual essences. At a very fundamental level of human existence, gratitude seems to be the symbolic way to make people understand that they are part of nature, actors in natural cycles of taking riches from the earth and giving back the appropriate returns. Throughout history people have had some understanding that what nature gives them is influenced by what they give nature. The ecological idea often takes on religious, spiritual, or magical connotations. Whether it is nature, *hau*, or God, the essential concept is gratitude, or the need to restore some equilibrium. The notion of a cycle of gifts that have to be kept in motion by passing them on or the idea of abundance returning only if due respect is paid is indicative of the same basic idea that life can only be safeguarded if we pass on what we have received. To come and remain alive means to give away.

The moral and psychological aspects of gratitude constitute the second layer. Gratitude can be conceived as a feeling of moral indebtedness as a consequence of what has been received. We have seen that this feeling has its roots in early childhood, where its first manifestation is the experience of a child's joy, comparable with the celebration of de Waal's chimps. Joy is the child's reaction to the first gift of motherly care and love and paves the way for gratitude. Although in later life the experience of gratitude may vary according to the extent to which one is dependent on others for the satisfaction of one's needs, the talent for gratitude can be considered an enduring personality trait and a moral virtue. Interestingly, the ability to receive and be grateful seems intrinsically related to its counterpart, the ability to return goodness, or generosity.

Whatever the impact of psychological factors, we should bear in mind that from its inception gratitude is embedded in social relationships. One might say that to give is to live, not only as an individual but also as a member of society. Not being grateful ultimately means the discontinuation of social bonds and community life and the termination of individual well-being and satisfaction. This, then, is the third layer of gratitude; it is the precondition for reciprocity and mutual exchange. As the anthropological literature on gift exchange amply demonstrates, gratitude keeps social relations intact by being the driving force behind the return gifts. Gratitude is the in-between connecting gift and return gift. Together the three elements of gift, gratitude, and countergift form the chain that constitutes the principle of reciprocity. The social view of gratitude may also involve some negative aspects. Power can seriously threaten the capacity to feel and express gratitude. Giving in return is not always inspired by

The Gift: Meanings and Motives

TABLE 3.1. Manifestations and Layers of Gratitude

Manifestations of Gratitude	Layers of Gratitude
Hau, the "spirit" of the gift, nature expecting returns	Spiritual/religious/magical/ecological
Joy and the capacity to receive	Moral/psychological
Mutuality, reciprocity, power inequality, fear of sanctions	Social
Culturally varying expressions but also web of feelings connecting people	Societal/cultural

pure gratitude but can also be motivated by a fear of social sanctions or of the discontinuation of profits ensuing from social relationships. Only in more or less equally balanced relationships can gratitude unfold the best of its powers.

The fourth layer consists of the societal and cultural meaning of gratitude. As Simmel stated, a culture or society deprived of all acts of gratitude will inevitably break down. Just as gratitude is indispensable in the life of one individual, who will face isolation and loneliness if his or her capacity to feel grateful is impaired, gratitude is also a crucial ingredient of every society and culture. Without the ties created by gratitude there would be no mutual trust, no moral basis on which to act, and no grounds for maintaining the bonds of community.

Table 3.1 summarizes the various ways gratitude may be expressed in people's experience and behavior, as well as the conceptual "layers" belonging to a particular manifestation of gratitude. The four layers or meanings of gratitude are not mutually exclusive. On the contrary, they are different formulations of the same force that compels people to restore the disequilibrium caused by having received a gift, whether from a supernatural power, nature, or a fellow human being. In all these cases, the failure to reciprocate acts as a boomerang to the recipients themselves, because the fundamental principle of gift giving – keeping gifts in motion by passing them on – is not heeded.

The enormous psychological, social, and cultural effectiveness of gratitude is based on the same capacity of mutual recognition that was involved in the act of gift giving itself (see Chapter 2). No gratitude can exist without recognition of the entity – person or nature – that brought the feelings of gratitude into existence. These insights play a crucial role in the theoretical model presented in Chapter 9.

In the words of Lewis Hyde (1983 [1979]: 50), "Those who will not acknowledge gratitude or who refuse to labour in its service neither free their gifts nor really come to possess them."

∽

FOUR

Women, Gifts, and Power

It is not that agents "create" the asymmetry; they enact it. In summary: being active and passive are relative and momentary positions; in so far as the relevant categories of actors are "male" and "female" then either sex may be held to be the cause of the other's acts; and the condition is evinced in the perpetual possibility of the one being vulnerable to the exploits of the other or able to encompass the other. The conclusion must be that these constructions do not entail relations of permanent domination.

(Marilyn Strathern 1988: 333–334)

Since Mauss and Malinowski the concept of "the gift" has been one of the main issues in anthropological research in non-Western cultures. An important question is whether gender plays any role in practices of gift exchange and, if so, what the nature of this role might be. The older anthropological contributions seem to be based on the assumption that women do not have any significant role in gift exchange. While Malinowski recognizes that women take a prominent part in certain ceremonial actions (1950 [1922]: 37), he does not mention any active female part in gift exchange; all his examples involve men. Writing some decades after Malinowski, Lévi-Strauss (1961 [1949]) draws attention to the practice occurring in many non-Western societies, that of exchanging women as the supreme gift. The prohibition of incest functions as a rule of reciprocity among men offering their sisters as marriage partners to other men outside their own clan. The exchange of women is described by Lévi-Strauss as being at the base of systems of kinship relations. Men, in his account, primarily see women as objects of gift exchange but not as subjects. Western anthropologists have usually interpreted the apparent absence of women as autonomous actors in gift exchange as a sign of the hierarchical dominance of men over women in Melanesia. As Marilyn Strathern argues in *The Gender of the Gift* (1988), however, this interpretation is biased by Western preconceptions. In Melanesia no permanent relations of dominance exist between men and women. Rather, women and men are alternatively subject or object for each other in their efforts to create and sustain social relations by means of gift exchange.

This raises the question what the role of power is in women's gift exchange. We already know from Chapter 2 that gifts are not exclusively friendly acts, springing from sympathy or love, but may also be conscious or unconscious vehicles to exercise power. How power is exactly involved in acts of gift exchange is not entirely clear, though. Power comes to be expressed in several facets of the phenomenon of gift exchange. I would think of the following possibilities (certainly not an exhaustive enumeration). First, giving extravagantly may be a means to obtain or affirm power and prestige, as Malinowski's fieldwork on the Trobriand Islands has shown. Second, receiving a gift brings about feelings of dependence and gratitude. Georg Simmel points to the fact that gratitude is not only morally obliging but also opens up the possibility of moral or other dominance by the giver over the recipient; for example, in gift giving power may be exercised by keeping the other indebted, or by demanding favors from the person in debt. Third, in the act of refusing or rejecting a gift, power is at stake because the refuser's definition of the situation – no continuation of the gift relationship – is imposed to the giver; not only the gift is refused but also the identity of the giver.

These three instances of the exercise of power by means of gift giving are mainly of a psychological nature, in that individual characteristics, assets, or feelings are involved. But gift exchange may also include sociological power characteristics. A fourth example, then, is that of reciprocal gift exchange functioning as a principle of exclusion by – consciously or unconsciously – affirming ties between the members of one's own group, and excluding others from participation within networks of mutual gift giving. And, fifth, the structural characteristics of the gift relationship may be such that reciprocity is not equivalent, for example, when one party feels obliged to give much with low expectations of return, whereas the other, more powerful party feels entitled to receive much without having to give much in return. In such cases the resources both parties dispose of are of unequal material or immaterial value.

From Annette Weiner's book *Women of Value, Men of Renown* (1976) it appears that this applies to women's and men's positions in Papua New Guinea: women and men perform activities in different domains and dispose of different types of resources from which their respective power positions emanate. Weiner attempts to redress the picture arising from Malinowski's work, of women as playing no role of any importance in gift exchange. Like Malinowski, Weiner collected her data on the Trobriand Islands. She shows that women are not exclusively the objects of gift exchange by men, as Claude Lévi-Strauss had suggested, but have an important and autonomous part in it. It appears from her research that gift giving occurs not only within but also between genders. Weiner clearly relates women's role in gift exchange to power and seems to conceive of power as a means of control over people and resources: "We must push exchange beyond the level of our view of the social world and seek to understand exchange as the means, however limited, of gaining power over people and control over resources in the widest sense" (1976: 220).

More recently, Weiner (1992) points to an important category of possessions, which may shed a new light on theories of reciprocity, and the role of power within these theories. She calls these possessions inalienable because they must not be given or, if they are circulated, must return finally to the giver (see Chapter 3). According to Weiner, "keeping-while-giving" is the fundamental drive underlying gift exchange, reciprocity merely being a superficial aspect of it. Inalienable possessions invariably share a general symbolism associated with the cosmological domains of human reproduction and cultural reproduction of the kin group. Cloth is an example of such an inalienable possession. Women, being the main producers and owners of cloth in most Oceania societies, play a pivotal part in the process of keeping-while-giving. Women's role in this domain is of key political significance, because power, or the (re)production of rank and hierarchy, is intimately involved in cultural reproduction. Women's autonomous share in gift exchange, their ownership of inalienable possessions, and their attendant strategical power position have remained unrecognized by most anthropologists.

One notable exception is the Dutch anthropologist van Baal (1975), who, as early as in the 1970s, attempted to redress the view shared by many anthropologists – and particularly Lévi-Strauss – of women as the passive objects of exchange processes between men, denying them any subjectivity of their own. Van Baal emphasizes the tremendous importance of women, not only as bearers of children but also as providers of motherly care and succor. This makes women immensely valuable to society in general and to men in particular. A woman, then, is not passively given away but agrees to be given away in marriage to a man of another group because she, being the "wife to the one and sister to the other, has manoeuvred herself into an intermediary position allowing her to manipulate. Two men protect her. The one owes a debt to the other and the other owes one to her" (van Baal 1975: 76).

Women's role in gift exchange in Western society has not been the focus of much research. The few studies that do exist, however, show unequivocally that women not only give more gifts than men – material as well as nonmaterial ones – but are also the greatest recipients. Which meaning should be attached to women's greater gift giving? How do these empirical findings relate to anthropological theories about women's power position in the domains of human and cultural reproduction? Can we learn anything from these theories with regard to women, gifts, and power in Western society? It is not immediately clear how we should interpret Western women's greater gift giving. To say that women are more altruistic than men is too simple and superficial. Empirical research does not show any substantial gender differences in altruism (Schwartz 1993). Gift giving by women is embedded in a network of social expectations, norms, and rules regarding their societal rights and duties and their position within the family. On certain domains women's social position in Western societies is still subordinate to that of men. The embeddedness of feminine liberality in persistent patterns of social inequality between genders suggests that women, gifts, and power are somehow related to each other. However, women's gift giving might not be as unequivocally or unambiguously related to power inequality as we are inclined to think when we depart from women's object status and subordinate position in Western society. Anthropological theories like Weiner's may contribute to deemphasize this focus on women's social subordination and to create room for other, less one-dimensional and more sophisticated interpretations.

In this chapter, the meaning of women's greater gift giving in Western society is explored by connecting it to social power inequality between genders. First, some of our own empirical results are presented insofar as they concern gender (Komter and Schuyt 1993a; 1993b). On the basis of these results, I argue that altruism is not a plausible explanation of women's more active role in gift giving. Second, I try to clarify the relationship between women's gift giving and power by suggesting four different models of reciprocity, in which the relative benefits from women's gift giving accruing to men and women differ. The outcome of this analysis proves to be more ambiguous than the power perspective suggests in the first place.

TABLE 4.1. Gifts Given or Received according to Gender (%)

	Given/Received	
	Women	Men
Presents	90/75	84/55
Money	85/58	84/49
Food	74/62	66/56
Stay	71/42	59/39
Care/help	73/62	58/48

Source: Komter and Schuyt (1993b).

Empirical Research on Women's Gift Giving

From both Caplow's and Cheal's studies discussed in Chapter 2, it appears that women are the greater givers, a finding that is corroborated by our own research. Our results show that small but consistent gender differences exist in the percentages of women and men who report having given presents, food, stay, and care or help to others; as to the amount of money gifts, women and men do not differ (see Table 4.1). The average time spent in devising and choosing a present, whether it was bought or made at home, was about half an hour; men take nine minutes longer than women to find the right gift. Furthermore, men more often have the feeling that they are giving more than they receive (49% and 26%, respectively). Men experience less reciprocity in their gift exchange relationships than women do. An interesting finding is that the discontent about the balance of giving and receiving is greatest with those categories of respondents who report to have given the least – men, those with less education, and elderly people. They do indeed receive less compared with the other categories of respondents, but the difference with respect to what they give is not necessarily greater than it is among the other categories.

In a secondary analysis of the research data, we controlled for gender differences in income, education, and occupational level. Women keep giving more than men, regardless of socioeconomic differences. Also there are no differences among women themselves: women who do not live in a traditional family situation and women who are employed give as much as women who have children, live with a partner, and do not have a paid job (unpublished data).

Presents and Money Gifts

As concerns the amount of gifts given and received during the preceding month, again women appear to give and receive more than men do. In one month women give an average amount of 3.5 gifts while receiving 2.8 gifts on average. The corresponding figures for men are 2.6 (given) and 2.2 (received). The majority of our respondents give and receive gifts, the value of which does not exceed €9. Expensive gifts, though given, are rather exceptional. To be sure, men give fewer but more expensive gifts compared with women. On average men have spent almost €27 on gifts during the preceding month, whereas women spent around €17. Although men receive fewer gifts than women, these gifts are more expensive. The average monetary value of gifts received by men during the preceding month amounts to €59.4; for women, the value is about half this amount: €31.4.

More than two-thirds of our respondents have given money gifts to the church, acquaintances, family, partner, or children, with children, church, and partners receiving the greatest amounts. With money gifts, the same pattern shows up as with "normal" gifts: men usually give fewer gifts, but their monetary value is greater than that of women's money gifts (€61.2 and €49.9, respectively). Again, men appear to receive fewer gifts but ones of greater value compared with women (€126.3 and €107.3, respectively).

A remarkable finding for which no easy interpretation is at hand is that the monetary value of gifts received (both monetary and nonmonetary) is higher than the value of the gifts given; this seems to contradict the outcome that the number of gifts received is smaller than the number of gifts given. Are we inclined to forget or underestimate what we spend on gifts ourselves, or do we overestimate the monetary value of gifts received? But how would that connect to the smaller number of received gifts? Unfortunately, on the basis of our research data it is not possible to answer these questions. An obvious explanation for the fact that women's gifts have a lower monetary value compared with men's gifts is that men have a higher average income than women so that they have more to spend.

Hospitality

Women more often invite other people to dinner than men do, and are invited more frequently by others as well. The same pattern applies to offering a stay in one's house and staying with others oneself: women offer and receive more of this type of hospitality than men. Offering one's house to other people temporarily is for most people a matter of course, if enough space is available. With dinners this is different. Some dinners are merely serving sociable ends by offering the opportunity for the exchange of friendly feelings, or moral or practical support to other people. On other occasions, however, feelings of being obliged to others prevail: many dinners serve to keep family or friendship ties alive, or to fulfill one's duty to reciprocate. Hospitality, then, is not a purely altruistic giving activity. Nothing is more obliging than being invited to dinner. It is therefore very unlikely that the cycle of gift and return gift is closed after one round.

Care and Help

We distinguished the following types of care and help: doing small jobs for others, caring for the sick or the elderly, giving psychological support, helping people to move, helping with transport (e.g., transporting children to and from school), and participating in (unpaid) management or administrative activities. Again, women are the ones who care and help the most. Doing small jobs and helping people to move are activities more often performed by men, but women offer all other types of care or help more frequently than men do. As was the case with hospitality, offering care or help does not necessarily or mainly spring from altruistic motives. The motives lie scattered on an imaginary scale of altruism: from selflessly wanting to contribute to the well-being of other people, without any expectations of return, to reciprocally exchanging help or helping as a compensation for being helped oneself, to keeping a sharp eye as to whether the debt balance is not pending too much to one side. You are helping other people, knowing that you will be helped in return.

Blood and Organs

Of our respondents 31% have given blood. More men than women have given blood (38% and 25%, respectively), whereas women are the greater recipients of blood. We should be aware of the fact that men are allowed to give blood more often than women for medical reasons – four and three times a year, respectively. That women receive more blood may be related to their greater needs as a result of pregnancy and childbirth. However, more women than men have considered giving blood: 49% and 30%, respectively. Apparently, women's willingness to give blood is relatively great but the restrictions to donation reduce participation. Of our respondents 26% have made up an organ codicil, with female respondents outranking their male counterparts (31% and 21%, respectively).

There are some doubts about Titmuss's view of blood donations as the "free" and altruistic gift par excellence (Titmuss 1970). For some of our respondents the main motive to give blood was "having a free afternoon from military service." Often a kind of postponed reciprocity is involved. One respondent says: "It can happen to me too, such an accident. You may be in need of blood yourself, at some time, and then you are lucky that there are some other people who have given their blood." Perhaps the bearers of an organ codicil are the true altruists.

It is justified, on the basis of these data, to claim that women are the greater givers compared with men. Even though the monetary value of the gifts they give is lower compared with that of men's gifts (women have less to spend), women give not only more normal gifts but also more nonmaterial gifts than men do. Women's liberality is consistent over all gift objects we distinguished in the research. Moreover, the results of our study are confirmed by the findings concerning women's larger share in gift giving, reported by Caplow and Cheal. However, women appear to be the greatest recipients as well. The principle of reciprocity is the most likely explanation for this. Motives to give seem to be mainly a mixture of altruistic feelings and expectations of return, as discussed in Chapters 1 and 2. And even when gifts are given altruistically, it is assumed that people end up with some self-reward from their unselfish gift giving, for example a positive feeling about themselves – a phenomenon that has been called the altruistic paradox.

How are we to explain women's greater liberality compared with men's? It is unlikely that women are simply blessed with a greater level of altruism than men are. Gifts may convey symbolic meanings that do not so much harmonize with altruism but rather express thoughtlessness, indifference, criticism, a need for attention, or an attempt to seduce. In fact, the results of our research showed that gifts of this type are no exceptions. Altruism and gift giving are often very indirectly related, if at all. As we will see in Chapters 6 and 7, motives to offer care or help to other people are often disinterested as well as selfish. The explanation for women's liberality should rather be sought in different sets of expectations regarding women and men, normative conceptions of what gender roles should consist of, and in differences in the cultural and social value attributed to women's and men's main domains of activity. All this should then be considered against the background of factual inequality in women's and men's social positions, which becomes manifest in their differing material and nonmaterial resources (e.g., participation in paid work, income, participation in informal networks, occupying leading positions, amount of free time).

There are good reasons to assume that power inequality between genders is implied in women's gift giving, but the question is what this relationship looks like: who is benefiting most from women's greater gift giving? Are women affirming their own status or power position, or even gaining in power by means of their giving, just like the inhabitants of the Trobriand Islands? Or are women the net losers of their own gift giving because it is merely what is expected from them as females and amounts to the reproduction of their subordinate position in society?

Four Models to Interpret Women's Gift Giving

The focus of the four models to be presented here is on the structural inequality in social power between women and men, their different types of resources, and the differential social value attributed to these. Women's gift exchange in our Western society might be related to power in the four following ways: asymmetrical reciprocity in favor of men, in which men are supposed to benefit most from women's liberality; equivalent reciprocity, in which women and men benefit equally by their respective giving, albeit on different domains; asymmetrical reciprocity in favor of women, in which women themselves benefit most by their important role in gift giving; and alternating asymmetry, in which women and men profit alternatively from the dominant and gendered pattern of gift giving.

Asymmetrical Reciprocity in Favor of Men

Reciprocal exchange is often mistaken for symmetrical exchange in the sense that both parties exchange goods of about equal value. Under the surface of reciprocity, however, very asymmetrical forms of exchange and even pure exploitation may be hidden: "[E]verywhere in the world the indigenous category for exploitation is 'reciprocity'" (Sahlins 1972: 134). Reciprocity, then, is not synonymous with symmetry or equivalence. One can speak of equivalent exchange only when both parties in an exchange relationship have rights as well as duties toward each other and exchange goods of about equal value. Many anthropological studies about gift exchange seem to confirm the model of "asymmetrical reciprocity in favor of men": men are the dominant parties in gift giving, and prevailing patterns of gift exchange benefit men more than women; men are reported to assert dominance over women by demanding obedience and ignoring women's concerns (Strathern 1988).

When women do not, or barely, take part in gift exchange (as Malinowski wrongly assumed), this may be a manifestation of their subordinate role in a certain society. But also when women do have a substantial share in gift giving, as in our own society, this may be interpreted as a sign of their subordination. Women's liberality in Western society may be explained in terms of asymmetrical reciprocity in favor of men because it reinforces and reproduces the hierarchically ordered division of labor and the unequal power relationship between genders. The domain of the market economy with its formally regulated patterns of exchange prevails over the domain of the informal gift economy in terms of power and prestige. In this model women's greater share in giving gifts is related to their position within the family and their traditional responsibility for maintaining social contacts. As "kinkeepers" (Rosenthal 1985) women are expected to keep a good record of birthdays, wedding days, and other festivities, or to visit ill people, and to buy the appropriate presents. Because of these expectations, women can barely escape their gift giving duties, whether they like them or not. Historically speaking, there are good reasons to assume that the significance of women's gift giving has even increased during the past decades: the relative stability of social and familial networks is diminishing as a consequence of an increased divorce rate and of the growing geographical distances that separate people's domiciles (van Leer 1995). From this perspective reinforcing social ties through gift giving is more needed than ever.

Up to a certain extent the dominant gender relationships and stereotypes force women's liberality upon them. In this model giving is a form of – not entirely voluntary – labor performed by women merely serving to affirm their inferior social position.

Equivalent Reciprocity

It is also possible that exchange relationships imply different but complementary power resources to women and men. What women and men give is different but yet equivalent. This would be a case of equivalent reciprocity. Weiner (1976) gives an example of such an interpretation of gift exchange by women in a non-Western society. She shows that the Trobriand women were especially active as givers of gifts on the occasion of rituals concerning the cycle of life and death. Women play an outstanding role in the regeneration of *dala*, the transmission of the identity of the nameless and anonymous ancestors who are assumed to have "the same blood" and come from the same place and the same country (Weiner 1976: 253). Women envelop their child in a towel, bind it to a stick, and put the stick in the soil where they are laboring. They hope that the ancestors' spirit will thus enter into the child through the soil and the stick. In the experience of the Trobriand inhabitants the essence of persons and their spirit is transmitted by women. According to Weiner, women therefore dispose of an important form of power and control, namely the control over the ahistoric, cosmic, timeless phenomena of life and death. Men derive their power and control from another domain, that of material possessions and wealth, concrete gifts like yams, arm shells, and necklaces – the famous Kula gifts described by Malinowski – to concrete persons. This domain is, much more than that of women, situated in historical time and space. The gifts men give to each other derive their value, among others, from the fact that they inherited them from famous and respected persons. By giving precious goods to each other, men create relationships between specific individuals over different generations. Weiner concludes that women as well as men dispose of important power resources, but each does so in a different domain.

Are these ideas relevant to our own culture? Of course, our market economy has replaced the former gift economy to a certain extent (not completely, though, as the gift economy still exists alongside the market economy). And, of course, our culture radically differs from the one of the Trobriand inhabitants. Nevertheless, some parallels with Weiner's findings may be drawn. The market is the domain where men still are in possession of most power resources: they are playing the most active role in the exchange of money and commodities. The informal exchange of gifts outside the market is mainly the domain of women. Arguing from the model of symmetrical reciprocity, men and women derive equivalent power from their respective exchange transactions. By means of their giving gifts, women function as the guardians of social relationships. Women and their gifts are, so to speak, the "greasing oil" of our society, without which the human machinery would certainly break down. In contrast, men are in large part responsible for economic transactions. The big money is mainly circulating through their hands, and also the "greasing money" – monetary bribery – is still predominantly a male affair. The economic domain of commodity production and exchange offers many possibilities to acquire power and prestige. Analogously to Weiner's reasoning, however, women would have another but equally important domain of exchange transactions from which to derive power: interpersonal interaction, the social machinery where everything has to run smoothly as well. The exchange of economically not "useful" but symbolically rich and socially indispensable gifts by women would, then, equal the economically useful exchange of commodities performed mainly by men. In the latter type of exchange, the social and symbolic meaning is subordinate to the economic one.

Asymmetrical Reciprocity in Favor of Women

Although Weiner interprets her own findings as a case of what I called "symmetrical reciprocity," another interpretation is possible as well. The symbolic control the Trobriand women were exerting over the cosmic cycle of life and death may be regarded as a much more fundamental source of power than the kind of power that ensues from men's historically, temporally, and spatially restricted, concrete, and specific forms of gift exchange. The transmission of *dala* is, in the end, a precondition of all other forms of gift exchange. When one is insecure about the continuity of the ancestral spirit, actual, competitive gift exchange between men may not even be possible at all. The preservation of existing ties and the formation of new ones may become problematic in that case.

In our Western world, too, one might consider women's important role in gift exchange as an indispensable investment in the social fundament of our society. This social fundament can be considered as being more basic than the economic fundament. Without a certain amount of kindness and benevolence in relationships between people, at home, at work, and in other kinds of social contexts, the survival chances of the market economy are in jeopardy. Economic life can simply not dispense with forms of institutionalized or noninstitutionalized kindness: the "human factor" cannot be left out.

Without suggesting that this role is, or should be, the exclusive prerogative of women, the well-known gender differences do play a role here. Not every woman has social skills, and many men are as socially skilled as women, but in everyday practice concern for the human factor and the capacity to transform this concern into concrete acts of benevolence are often found in women. They are the ones who buy flowers for ill colleagues and toys for newborn babies. They are the binding factor on the yearly "day out" with one's colleagues. They keep an eye on the personal well-being of the people surrounding them and often act as intermediaries in case of conflicts. These acts of symbolic or material kindness toward others, in considerable part performed by women, are indispensable for maintaining a livable world.

Women's greater share in gift giving may, therefore, imply a relative advantage in terms of the social resources it offers them. Women indeed often have more and longer-lasting friendships than men, start new contacts more easily through school or neighborhood, are more often concerned about their family members, and therefore develop more intensive family ties compared with men. Although business connections benefit men more in terms of economic resources, women's personal relations offer them more social and human advantage. In the end, this last type of advantage might prove to be more important than any economic profit: in times of personal problems, illness, death, or other misery, a business connection is of no great use. After all, our personal happiness is more dependent on interpersonal than on economic factors, if a certain level of economic resources is guaranteed.

In this third model, women's liberality brings the greatest benefit to themselves. The asymmetric pattern of gift exchange existing between genders advantages women more than men, not only because they receive the greatest amount of gifts but also, and mainly, because of the benevolence and kindness symbolized in these gifts, and the social benefit this implies. Giving by women turns back to themselves as a pleasurable kind of boomerang.

Alternating Asymmetry

None of the models discussed thus far is entirely satisfying. Women do not give exclusively because their traditional role urges them to do so (the first model) but also because they want to give and derive pleasure from it. Another problem is that the forms of power women and men can derive from their respective domains are not equivalent (the second model). The two domains are associated with different possibilities for societal participation, different socioeconomic positions, and differences in acquired jobs, incomes, and prestige. Informal gift exchange by women may certainly be an important complement to formal market exchange by men, but the type and amount of power associated with these two forms of exchange are not necessarily equal or equivalent. Although women's gift giving undeniably yields them some social benefits (the third model), the big question is again what this finally amounts to in terms of economic and political power. In order to be able to share in these types of power, a greater part in economic exchange seems necessary.

In devising the fourth model I took my inspiration from Marilyn Strathern (1988). Strathern criticizes the usual Western interpretation of the relationship between women and men in Melanesian culture in terms of hierarchical patterns of dominance. In Western thinking the collective and the familial sphere are ordered hierarchically. Melanesian people experience these as equivalent. Western people regard humans as internally consistent entities, whereas Melanesian men and women consider persons as composed of different parts. Melanesians do not think in terms of "structures" or "values" determining the behavior of individual men and women: "[I]t is agents, not systems who act" (Strathern 1988: 328). A person interprets only the concrete behavior or actions of another person, and not cultural conventions, as the cause of his or her own behavior. The idea that masculine values in a certain culture are the cause of feminine subordination is at odds with this way of thinking and experiencing the surrounding world. Our familiar oppositions between object and subject, passive and active, and the idea of persons as consistent entities do not apply in the Melanesian context. According to Strathern, then, it is a mistake to regard men and women as either active object or passive subject of interpersonal transactions. Melanesian men and women experience each other as the cause of their own actions. Men and women take themselves, as it were, as an aspect of the social identity of the other sex. A woman who is exchanged by men is not necessarily reduced to an object by this act. Rather, she is a link in the chain of relationships, while preserving her own autonomy.

These more or less equivalent acts of exchange may exist alongside evident forms of male dominance such as violence against women (and other men) that, according to Strathern, also exist in Melanesian culture. Her conclusion is, however, that in Melanesia no permanent relations of dominance exist between men and women. Rather, women and men are alternatively subject or object for each other in their continuing efforts to create and sustain social relations. Although every act contains an element of inherent force in its consequences for other people and does, therefore, generate temporary asymmetry in the interaction, this asymmetry is not permanent but is alternated by a form of asymmetry where the roles of object and subject, of active and passive, are reversed.

Even though Strathern's conception of women's autonomy in Melanesia may sound overly optimistic in view of the patterns of male dominance and force that she describes as well, her contention that our traditional Western schemes of one-sided, hierarchical dominance of men over women are not valid when applied to Melanesian culture should be taken seriously. It might also prove useful to abandon these schemes – characteristic of many feminist analyses of the 1970s – when thinking about women's status in Western society.

Strathern developed her views in order to understand the essence of Melanesian culture. Nevertheless, these views may also be applicable to gift exchange by women in Western society. The relationship between women, gifts, and power might be interpreted as characterized by alternating asymmetry. I mean by this that the first and the third models are alternating: women and men alternatively benefit from the fact that women are the greater givers. The second model – which presupposes symmetry of domains – is not valid because the different kinds of exchange transactions of women and men are not equivalent with regard to the societal power associated with them. However, the first model – men benefit the most from women's informal giving – cannot be rejected so easily. Men are indeed often relatively well off as a result of women's liberality but this is not the whole and not necessarily the only correct story. Also the third model – giving by women is the most profitable for themselves – contains some truth.

With alternating benefits, I do not mean a sort of chronological alternation – first model 1, and then model 3, or the reverse. The concept rather points to the fact that the benefits of gift giving alternate from one party to the other, depending on the perspective that is chosen and on the specific circumstances in which the giving occurs. As concerns the *perspective*, women's (and men's) social reality has different faces. Being constrained by the burden of traditional household tasks and duties is one; deriving pleasure from giving gifts to other people, receiving much in return, and having ample social relations constitute another face. The former does not exclude the latter, and both can even exist simultaneously. Regarding the *circumstances*, although giving in extreme amounts and with extreme intensity is probably not psychologically healthy because of the risk of losing one's self (gift giving is giving "something of one's own self"), some women want or are actually obliged to do this. A constellation of psychological tendencies to be self-sacrificing and to obliterate oneself, particularly when combined with a strongly asymmetric power relationship between genders, certainly promotes the dominance of the first model. In that case women's liberality mainly benefits others (for instance, men) and predominantly impacts their own costs. On the contrary, the third model becomes prevalent when women already dispose of certain important power resources, for example, in the form of economic independence and psychological autonomy. When this is the case, the traditionally female caring for the quality of social relationships by means of gift giving may turn out to be advantageous for women because the social capital it generates tends to accumulate: the more one has, the more one gets. This applies to relationships as well as to gifts, which prove to be inextricably linked.

The fact that women in Western society are the greatest givers, then, cannot be disentangled, on the one hand, from their more vulnerable societal and economic position compared with that of men and, on the other hand, from the power they are invested with by being society's prime intermediaries in creating and recreating social relationships by means of gift giving.

If this fourth model has some validity, it means that different interpretations of the meaning of women's gift exchange are needed for different categories of women. Moreover, even within one woman's life gift giving may have different meanings. That women in our society have such a substantial share in gift giving should not too easily be attributed to either some altruistic disposition or to their social subordination. Although the amount of women's gift exchange may strongly correlate with their traditional feminine role as Cheal (1988) has suggested, the meaning of their gift giving seems to vary with their personal and social circumstances.

The Paradox of Female Gift Giving

In contrast to our usual thinking, giving is inherently asymmetrical. Power may be involved in gift giving in several ways. Gifts may enhance personal status or power. They create a relationship of debt and dependency between giver and recipient in which the possibility of power abuse is always present. Gifts, and with them the identity of the giver, may be refused. Gift giving to some people excludes others from the material and immaterial benefits implied in this practice. In gift exchange structural inequality of resources may be involved; on the basis of power inequality some people feel obliged to give much while receiving little, whereas others, though poor givers themselves, are endowed with abundant gifts.

How do women, as the greatest givers and recipients, come into this picture? In the light of the many possibilities to exercise power by means of gift giving, it is too easy and even misleading to consider women's greater liberality as the mere expression of noble feeling. In addition to affection, respect, or gratitude, also manipulation, flattering, or being in need of personal attention are common motives to give (of course, this applies to both genders). Women seem to be no exception when painful, hurting, or offending gifts are given and, after all, are not the most notorious poisoners in history of the female sex?

Another explanation draws upon structural power asymmetries between women and men and upon the difference in resources from which power may be derived. It is not clear which gender benefits most from women's liberality. On the one hand, women's gift giving may be considered as a manifestation of gendered power inequality, because this is what they are expected to do as housewives. Their liberality may turn against them, for example, when they sacrifice their own autonomy for the sake of others. On the other hand, giving by women entails many attractive benefits to themselves as well: closer relationships and more extended social networks, and, therefore, a greater chance to receive attention, care, or help from others when necessary. Moreover, women receive relatively many material gifts themselves, which is also a pleasant aspect. How the balance of benefits or disadvantages for women as greatest givers will exactly weigh out depends on their personal power resources and social circumstances.

Women's gift giving is caught in a fundamental paradox. On the one hand, their gift exchange may be considered a powerful means of affirming social identities and of creating and maintaining social relationships. Women's activity in this domain might be interpreted as an effort "to secure permanence in a serial world that is always subject to loss and decay" (Weiner 1992: 7). On the other hand, given their unequal societal and economic power compared with that of men, women incur the risk of losing their own identity by giving much to others. In the act of giving, women are simultaneously creating the opportunity to keep or gain power, and making themselves vulnerable to the loss of power and autonomy. Weiner's idea about "keeping-while-giving" – exchanging things in order to keep them – is a perfect illustration of this paradoxical tension in women's gift giving: to overcome the threats of loss – of their own selves, of their power vis-à-vis men, and of important social bonds – they give away abundantly. And, as a consequence of giving abundantly, they are facing the threat of losing their autonomy. It is as though men's greater societal and economic power not only renders it less urgent for them to engage in substantial gift giving but also protects them from loss of autonomy through giving to other people.

The gender difference in gift giving illustrates the substantial role of women in creating the social cement of society. Although many forms of solidarity are not gendered at all, this applies neither to gift giving nor to informal care, a type of solidarity that is discussed in Chapters 6 and 7. Despite their increased emancipation, women still have the largest share in informal care. In these cases solidarity is clearly related to gender.

PART II

Solidarity and Selectivity

∞

FIVE

Social Theory and Social Ties

As to the question which gave rise to this work, it is that of the relations between the individual personality and social solidarity. What explains the fact that, while becoming more autonomous, the individual becomes more closely dependent on society? How can he simultaneously be more personally developed and more socially dependent? For it is undeniable that these two developments, however contradictory they may seem, are equally in evidence. That is the problem which we have set ourselves. What has seemed to us to resolve this apparent antinomy is a transformation of social solidarity due to the steadily growing development of the division of labour.

(Emile Durkheim 1964a [1893]: 37–38)

How is social order created? How is social order maintained? What makes people live together in peace and initiate mutual ties? What are the origins of the trust that is needed to be able to exchange goods and services? What are the psychological, social, and cultural conditions for the development of social ties? Those are the old questions to which social science – as advanced by its classical as well as its more modern authors – has attempted to find answers. The theme of social order has not exclusively been a central focus in the sociological discipline, but also in anthropology. In addition to Durkheim, Weber, and Parsons, who took primarily (but not exclusively) Western society as point of departure for their analyses, ethnologists and anthropologists such as Malinowski and Lévi-Strauss have studied the conditions for the genesis of a common culture. Processes of reciprocal exchange – of gifts, goods, and services – and the sense of moral obligation originating in these processes proved to be the basis of many non-Western societies.

In speaking of social order as a "problem," Talcott Parsons identifies two conditions at its root. First, people have limited capacities to sympathize with their fellow human beings: there is a constant tension between the moral obligations they feel toward other people and the impulse to promote their own interests. What is desirable from a normative perspective does not necessarily correspond to our actual needs, wishes, and desires; this may be called a moral shortage. Second, people inhabit an environment that provides insufficient resources to fulfill the needs of all members of society; here, a material shortage, a problem of scarcity, is involved. "The problem of order is ... rooted in inescapable conflict between the interests and desires of individuals and the requirements of society: to wit, the pacification of violent strife among men and the secure establishment of co-operative social relations making possible the pursuit of collective goals" (Wrong 1994: 36).

The more society is in a process of change, the more social science is concerned with the concepts of cohesion and solidarity. Therefore, it is not surprising that at the end of the nineteenth century sociologists were analyzing the consequences of the transition from traditional to modern society for social cohesion and solidarity and anthropologists were wondering on which principles culture and order in non-Western societies were based. Which were their main ideas, and what can we still learn from them? Why is the theory of the gift a theory of human solidarity?

Classical Theory: Unity of Generosity and Self-Interest

Affective and Instrumental Bases of Solidarity

According to Durkheim the nature of solidarity is the central problem of sociology. This is the thread that runs through his whole work: what are the ties uniting people to each other, he wondered in 1888, five years before he wrote *De la division du travail social*, where he elaborates his theory of solidarity (Lukes 1973).

Durkheim's predecessors had already developed some ideas about the social texture of society. In a work that predates Durkheim by a few decades, Auguste Comte, for instance, describes the social equilibrium in modern society as the result of the division.of labor and occupational specialization. But to Comte the principle of differentiation and specialization also is a threat to feelings of community and togetherness. In contrast to Comte, Herbert Spencer emphasizes the element of self-interest involved in solidarity. In accordance with the tradition of British utilitarianism and the thinking of Adam Smith, he regards social cohesion as the result of the undisturbed interplay of individual interests; no shared beliefs, norms, or state regulations are needed to realize cohesion and solidarity. Tönnies, the first to analyze the transformation of solidarity in the nineteenth century, describes how in the transition from *Gemeinschaft* to *Gesellschaft* the traditional community values as they were embodied in the small-scale social unities of family, neighborhood, and village were substituted by individualized feelings and needs. In the large-scale centralized nation-state, social relationships had become dominated by economic rationality and free competition between individual interests. In contrast to Spencer, Tönnies presents a gloomy picture of the rising capitalist society, which could only be kept under control by a strong state.

Durkheim agrees with Tönnies's division into two types of society, and also with his global characterization of *Gemeinschaft*. But while Tönnies describes *Gesellschaft* as a mechanical aggregate, Durkheim does not conceive of premodern societies as more "organic" than contemporary ones. According to him collective activity in more modern societies is as spontaneous and natural as in more small-scale communities. In the end Durkheim reverses Tönnies's terminology: he reserves the term "mechanical solidarity" for the human ties that characterize traditional societies, while using "organic solidarity" to describe modern forms of community. He explains his choice for these terms as follows: mechanical solidarity "does not signify that it is produced by mechanical and artificial means. We call it that only by analogy to the cohesion which unites the elements of an inanimate body, as opposed to that which makes a unity out of the elements of a living body." In the case of mechanical solidarity "the social molecules . . . can act together only in the measure that they have no actions of their own, as the molecules of inorganic bodies" (1964a [1893]: 130).

Mechanical solidarity corresponds to a "system of homogeneous segments that are similar to one another" (1964a [1893]: 181). Society comprises such segments (families, clans, and territorial districts), which are characterized by a very low degree of interdependence. There is no fundamental distinction between individuals. Individual conscience is dependent on the collective conscience, and individual identity is a part of group identity. In mechanical solidarity human behavior is regulated by the shared norms, sentiments, and values that form together the *conscience collective*. This type of solidarity is reflected in the application of severe penal sanctions – "repressive law" – to deviant behavior or the violation of norms. Religion is a dominant factor in social life, and the codes of morality are concrete and specific.

In more modern societies organic solidarity is gradually replacing mechanical solidarity. Organic solidarity is based on individual difference. The increased division of labor and occupational specialization at the end of the nineteenth century brought about a differentiation in societal tasks and functions comparable to the different functions of the bodily organs, which analogy explains Durkheim's "organic solidarity." Durkheim assumes a direct relationship between the degree of specialization of societal functions and the extent of social cohesion: the more labor is divided and the activity of each is specialized, "the stronger is the cohesion which results from this solidarity" (1964a [1893]: 131). Or, in his organ terminology, "the unity of the organism is as great as the individuation of the parts is more marked" (131). There is a high level of mutual dependency. Legal regulations determine the nature of and relationships between the different societal tasks and functions. As the division of labor extends, the conscience collective weakens: its content becomes increasingly secular and human-oriented, and morality is becoming more abstract and universal. It is important to bear in mind that Durkheim regards the distinction between the solidarity types as an analytical one and, in fact, as two aspects of the same reality that are rarely entirely separate.

In line with Tönnies's distinction between *Gemeinschaft* and *Gesellschaft* Max Weber distinguishes between communal and associative social relationships. When people's action – either individual or collective – is based on the subjective feeling of togetherness, Weber speaks of communal relationships. This feeling may stem from affection or from tradition, but it is essential that more than the mere feeling of togetherness is involved. "It is only when this feeling leads to a mutual orientation of their behaviour to each other that a social relationship arises between them" (1947 [1922]: 138). Associative relationships are at issue when the orientation of action springs from a rationally motivated correspondence between interests. This rationality may be inspired either by certain absolute values or by instrumental and utilitarian considerations. An example is market exchange, consisting of a compromise between opposed but complementary interests. Another example is the purely voluntary association between individuals on the basis of their self-interest; or the voluntary association of individuals sharing certain values.

Different from associative relationships, communal relationships have an affective, emotional, or traditional basis – for example, religious fraternities, erotic relationships, personal loyalty, or the esprit de corps within the military. The most typical communal relationship is the family, according to Weber. Most social relationships possess this affective component but are at the same time determined by associational factors. "No matter how calculating and hard-headed the ruling considerations in such a social relationship – as that of a merchant to his customers – may be, it is quite possible for it to involve emotional values which transcend its utilitarian significance" (1947 [1922]: 137). Like Durkheim Weber stresses the impossibility of a strict distinction between the different types of social relationship: they are ideal types. In everyday practice any social relationship that transcends the pursuit of immediate interests and is of a longer duration generates enduring social bonds, which cannot be reduced to mere utilitarian considerations. The reverse is also true: within communal relationships actions may sometimes be inspired by utilitarian motives.

The American sociologist Talcott Parsons is clearly inspired by these founding fathers of sociology (1952, 1977). For instance, Durkheim's emphasis on the contribution of common values to the integration of social systems can be recognized in *The Social System* (1952). In this book Parsons distinguishes loyalty from solidarity. He considers loyalty the noninstitutionalized precursor of solidarity: the individual motivation to conform to the interests or expectations of another person. Only when these expectations have become an institutionalized obligation can we speak of solidarity. Inasmuch as these roles are institutionalized, solidarity with the collectivity of which one is a part is involved. Also Parsons returns to Tönnies's terminology in his differentiation between certain types of collectivity: "A collectivity in which expressive interests have primacy in its orientation to continual action in concert may . . . be called a *Gemeinschaft*; one in which instrumental interests have primacy is an 'organization'" (1952: 100). Like Durkheim and Weber, Parsons acknowledges the possibility of mixtures between *Gemeinschaft* and *Gesellschaft*, for instance, in relationships between the incumbents of certain professional roles and their clients: universalism, functional specificity, and affective neutrality – characteristics of *Gesellschaft* – go along with the obligation implied in the profession to serve the community, irrespective of any financial considerations.

Parsons does not develop a full-blown theory of solidarity. However, he does have a clear-cut opinion on the basis of solidarity: "I should like to suggest that the primary 'cement' which makes such groups solidary is affective ties" (1952: 157). In the process of socialization within the family the child develops its first affective ties. This is the basis of the formation of an internalized capacity to affectivity that can be transferred to objects outside the family. Affectivity is, according to Parsons, a "generalized medium" comparable with money, power, and influence.

From these various sociological accounts two main types of solidarity come to the fore, whose bases are only seemingly in opposition to each other. They are brought together in the following scheme:

Gemeinschaft	*Gesellschaft*
mechanical solidarity	organic solidarity
communal relationships	associative relationships
expressive relationships	instrumental relationships

One may feel tempted to associate the left column with preindustrial society in which small homogeneous communities are tied together by strong feelings of solidarity, and to regard the right column as the prototype of modern solidarity as it has evolved in industrialized society. The underlying assumptions about human nature involve, on the one hand, *homo sociologicus*, the individual as embedded in small-scale social relationships, and whose solidary behavior is based on internalized moral obligations and, on the other hand, *homo economicus*, the rational, market-oriented individual, whose moral codes are abstract and universal. Solidarity is synonymous, here, with promoting the collective interest of mutually dependent individuals.

As we have seen, such a simplified dichotomy is not found in the works of the classical authors just discussed. Although most of them distinguish different types of solidarity, they all emphasize that these types are not mutually exclusive and, indeed, often occur together in varying combinations. The idea that the two types of solidarity do not exclude each other seems to have been lost in more modern theories, as I argue in a moment, after discussing some other classical anthropological and sociological contributions.

Reciprocity and Morality as Bases of Social Ties

Malinowski's detailed account of the Kula ritual – the pattern of ceremonial gift exchange among the population of the Trobriand archipelago discussed in Chapter 3 – describes a continuous gift exchange that takes place between the inhabitants of these islands. It follows a fixed pattern with articles of two kinds constantly traveling in opposite directions and constantly being exchanged. Every detail of the transactions is fixed and regulated by a set of rules and conventions. Most important is that the gifts keep moving through the archipelago: a gift should never stagnate. The issue is not the durable possession of certain articles but the principle of exchange itself. The ever continuing movement of the objects from one (temporary) owner to the next is crucial in the process of acquiring a personal and social identity, status, and prestige and of creating social ties.

Malinowski proposes a continuum of feelings involved in gift giving. Pure gifts, altruistic gifts for which nothing is expected in return, and gifts that can be characterized as barter or forms of exchange where personal profit is the dominant motive, are the exceptions. Most typical are motives that lie in between these extremes. More or less equivalent reciprocity, attended by clear expectations of returns, is the general rule underlying gift exchange. According to Malinowski this economic dimension of gift giving corresponds with the sociological dimension of kinship: gifts to kin and partners are more often given disinterestedly, whereas more or less direct expectations of returns and elements of barter are more characteristic of gifts given to persons farther away in the kinship hierarchy.

Like his master Durkheim, Marcel Mauss takes a critical stance toward the then prevailing utilitarian strands in political theory by emphasizing the values of altruism and solidarity. However, he goes beyond Durkheim's conceptions of solidarity as based on collective representations or on the mutual dependency implied in the division of labor, by discovering gift exchange as the mechanism that reconciles individual interests and the creation of a social system. Mauss radicalizes Malinowski's insights by stating that *do ut des* is the principal rule in all gift giving. In his view, there are no free gifts: "Generosity and self-interest are linked in giving" (1990 [1923]: 68). He considers gift exchange as a subtle mixture of altruism and selfishness. Customs of potlatch – rivalrous gift giving in order to gain status and power (see Chapter 1) – illustrate this mixture in its most extreme form. Giving is not only a material act but also a symbolic medium involving strong moral obligations to give in return. By means of giving mutually it becomes possible to communicate with other people, to help them, and to create alliances. Gift exchange is at the basis of a system of mutual obligations between people and, as such, functions as the moral cement of human society and culture, according to Mauss.

In a work written some decades later, Lévi-Strauss (1961 [1949]) develops these insights further by considering the principle of reciprocity as a social structure determining our values, feelings, and actions. This is illustrated, for example, by the exchange of women by men in some non-Western societies. The principle of reciprocity is not limited to so-called primitive societies but also applies to Western society, according to Lévi-Strauss. He mentions examples in the sphere of offering food and the exchange of presents at Christmas. Forms of potlatch occur in our own society as well; for instance, the exhibition of Christmas cards on our mantelpiece and the vanity of much gift giving exemplify the destruction of wealth as a means to express or gain prestige. Far from being neutral objects without any special symbolic value, gifts are "vehicles and instruments for realities of another order: influence, power, sympathy, status, emotion; and the skilful game of exchange consists of a complex totality of manoeuvres, conscious or unconscious, in order to gain security and to fortify one's self against risks incurred through alliances and rivalry" (1965: 86).

Lévi-Strauss makes the important distinction between "restricted exchange," involving only two partners, and "generalized exchange," which refers to a more complex structure of exchange relationships. The concept of generalized exchange has been reconsidered by Sahlins (1972), who distinguishes between "generalized," "balanced," and "negative" reciprocity and richly illustrates these different forms with ethnographic materials. In generalized reciprocity – the disinterested extreme – the expectation of returns is indefinite, and returns are not stipulated by time, quantity, or quality. Like Gouldner and Malinowski, Sahlins mentions the circle of near kin and loved ones as an example. Feelings of altruism and solidarity supposedly accompany this type of exchange. Balanced reciprocity is less personal and refers to direct and equivalent exchange without much delay. It is more likely in relationships that are more emotionally distant. Feelings of mutual obligation go together with balanced reciprocity. Sahlins describes negative reciprocity – the unsociable extreme – as the "attempt to get something for nothing" (1972: 195). He summarizes his model as "kindred goes with kindness," and "close kin tend to share, to enter in generalized exchanges, and distant and nonkin to deal in equivalents or in guile" (Sahlins 1972: 196, quoting Tylor).

Conscious or unconscious expectations of reciprocity not only bring social relations about; they also stabilize already existing relations by making them predictable to a certain extent. In his essay "Faithfulness and gratitude," Simmel (1950 [1908]) analyzes the moral and social importance of these two feelings for sustaining reciprocity in human relationships. The different psychological motives on which social relations can be based, such as love, hate, and passion, are in themselves not sufficient to keep these relations alive. Simmel considers faithfulness – a kind of loyalty or commitment – a necessary feeling contributing to the continuity of an already existing social relationship. Faithfulness is what he calls a "sociological feeling," oriented to the relation as such, in contrast to the more person-oriented feelings like love, hate, or friendship. Gratitude is, just like faithfulness, a powerful means to establish social cohesion, as has been argued in Chapter 3. This is why Simmel calls gift giving "one of the strongest sociological functions": without it society would not come about.

Also Alvin Gouldner explores the "norm of reciprocity" as a mechanism to start social relationships. This norm helps to create social interaction "for it can reduce an actor's hesitancy to be the first to part with his valuables and thus enable exchange to get underway" (1973a: 255). Although equivalence and mutuality can be powerful motives to exchange gifts, Gouldner, following Simmel, points to the fact that reciprocity does not necessarily mean equivalence. However, Gouldner goes further than Simmel by reflecting more explicitly on the complicating role of power in reciprocity relations and by elaborating it theoretically. As we have seen in Chapter 3, reciprocal exchange relationships may be very asymmetrical. In addition to the norm of reciprocity, Gouldner distinguishes the "norm of beneficence," or the norm of giving "something for nothing" (Malinowski's "free gift"): the expression of real altruism. This kind of giving is not a reaction to gifts received from others. It is a powerful correction mechanism in situations where existing social relationships have become disturbed, or where people need care or help. Paradoxically, says Gouldner, "There is no gift that brings a higher return than the free gift, the gift given with no strings attached. For that which is truly given freely moves men deeply and makes them most indebted to their benefactors. In the end, if it is reciprocity that holds the mundane world together, it is beneficence that transcends this world and can make men weep the tears of reconciliation" (1973b: 277).

Despite clear-cut differences in approach, Simmel, Malinowski, Mauss, Lévi-Strauss, Gouldner, and Sahlins all seem to stress the same point: gifts are the moral cement of culture and society. Although power may complicate the principle of reciprocity, the primordial meaning of gift exchange is to start or to stabilize social relationships. An interesting parallel with the ideas of Durkheim, Weber, and Parsons, who do not so much oppose but rather juxtapose communal and instrumental relationship types, is that self-interest and the creation of social order are not regarded as contradictory. Generosity and self-interest go hand in hand in gift exchange, and it is exactly this combination that fosters the development of social order.

Modern Theory: Splitting Up Affection and Utility

In more modern conceptualizations of solidarity, two approaches have come into existence, the one stressing instrumental and utilitarian motives, the other considering norms, values, and emotions as the bases of solidarity. Authors like Hechter (1987), Coleman (1986), Elster (1989), Raub (1997), Lindenberg (1998), and (very differently) de Swaan (1988) are representatives of the first tradition, whereas scholars such as Mayhew (1971) and Etzioni (1988) can be said to advance the second approach.

Solidarity and Rational Choice Theory

Rational choice theorists differ with regard to the centrality of the role of self-interest in their theories. Some allow for other motivations as well. John Elster (1989), for instance, thinks that, in addition to self-interest, altruism, envy, and social norms are also contributing to social order, stability, and cooperation. Other rational choice theorists, though, regard self-interest as the prevailing motivation in determining an actor's choices between various action possibilities. One of the best-known theories of solidarity based on this latter view of rational choice is Michael Hechter's.

In his *Principles of Group Solidarity* (1987) he objects to three sociological traditions of thinking about solidarity: the normativistic, functionalist, and structuralist vision.

The first perspective, embodied in the work of Durkheim and Parsons, considers order as the result of internalized group norms. From the functionalist perspective that Hechter associates, for instance, with Elster, solidarity is explained by the survival value of certain forms of solidary behavior, whereas in the structuralist vision certain societal structures – for instance, patterns of stratification – are seen as the cause of group solidarity. Marx and Simmel provide examples of this approach. In Hechter's view, none of these approaches can explain differences in the degree to which people feel tied to the group or under which conditions group members will or will not conform to their obligations toward the group. The starting point of his own rational choice approach of solidarity is that individuals are "bearers of sets of given, discrete, nonambiguous, and transitive preferences" (1987: 30). In a situation where they can choose between alternative possibilities of action, they will always choose that alternative that presumably brings them the greatest profit. As profit maximizers, rational individuals are supposed to behave coherently and to be goal-oriented; they are, in brief, "rational egoists." Institutions play a regulating role, because they keep control of individual behavior by means of the rules they have developed.

An important factor explaining the extent to which people feel tied to a group is their dependency on the group for the satisfaction of their needs. In its turn, dependency is influenced by the availability of alternative resources for need satisfaction, the available information about these resources, the costs involved in leaving the group, and the strength of the personal ties among group members. The greater the dependency of the members, the stronger the group ties and obligations felt toward the group. The strength of group ties, however, is not enough to explain solidary behavior. Solidarity presupposes that people are in fact committing themselves to the group's ends and do not become "free riders."

Compliance requires formal controls, a group's means to counteract free riding. The group must have sufficient resources in order to be able to punish or reward its members effectively depending on their contribution to the group.

A similar perspective is found in the work of Coleman (1986). How can individual interests be reconciled with collective rationality? Coleman and Fararo (1992: xi–xii) describe as the principal aim of rational choice theory "to understand how actions that are reasonable or rational for actors can combine to produce social outcomes, sometimes intended by actors, sometimes unintended, sometimes socially optimal, sometimes non-optimal." The Dutch tradition of theoretical sociology also departs from a rational choice perspective in its focus on the interdependency of actors and the intended and unintended consequences of their behavior. Raub (1997: 23) argues, for instance, that, if we assume that "actors act according to their interests and that the interests of actors are their own interests," people will coordinate their actions while acknowledging interdependency with other actors in order to reach their economic and social goals.

The tension between individual and collective interests and rationality is also central to de Swaan's study about the rise of collective forms of solidarity in Europe and the United States (1988). Which are the indirect consequences of the misfortunes of some people for others who do not suffer directly from these misfortunes? Using diverging theoretical perspectives like Elias's civilization theory and Olson's theory on the logic of collective action, de Swaan analyzes the historical process in which people have become more and more dependent on each other, and the implications of this process for social solidarity. As interdependency networks became more extended, ramified, and complex, the influence of people's actions on others who took part in the same networks increased. Greater mutual dependency implies that the needs of some – caused by poverty, illness, or a lack of education – come to represent a threat to others who suffer less from these misfortunes. Poverty, for instance, meant a threat to public order, epidemics were threatening the lives of healthy individuals as well, and low education involved the risk of social exclusion of some, and therefore social instability for all. Therefore, it was in the rational self-interest of the privileged citizens to contribute financially and to arrange collective welfare facilities. The general access of these collective goods and the risk of free riding and abuse were the reasons for the development of the system of state-based care where everybody is equally obliged to contribute to the collective good.

Norms, Values, and Emotions as Bases of Solidarity

A very different approach of solidarity states that people come to feel committed to each other because they experience mutual attraction and want to identify with others and act loyally toward them. Solidarity starts with feelings of mutual connectedness. This view can be found in the work of Mayhew (1971). According to him solidary behavior is often organized in certain institutions, which he calls "systems of solidarity." An example is the family. Its function is "encouraging, stabilising, and regulating patterns of attraction, repulsion, loyalty, and identity within a population" (1971: 68). But solidarity is not restricted to kinship systems. People feel solidarity with all sorts of communities, ethnic groups, groups of colleagues, religious groupings, or even nations. Mayhew distinguishes between four forms of solidarity. First is the primary ties of affection between people, or *attraction*. When a group member not only feels attracted to the group but also cares for the unity of the group and the group ends, *loyalty* is involved. The other two forms of solidarity are not so much based on direct emotional attachment to others but rather on a feeling of belonging to the group, or *identification*. Identification with a group often surpasses attraction or loyalty; for instance, people may identify with homosexuals, blacks, or people of higher education, as a group. The fourth form of solidarity is *association*; this solidarity transcends established group identities and distinctions. The latter two forms of solidarity correspond to Durkheim's organic solidarity, whereas the more direct attraction among individuals resembles his mechanical solidarity.

A related perspective can be found in Etzioni's work. In accordance with the communitarian tradition in American philosophy and social science, Etzioni (1988) pleads for the revaluation of "the moral dimension." He criticizes what he calls the neoclassical paradigm because it rests upon a rationalistic, utilitarian, and individualistic picture of human nature. This picture is wrong, says Etzioni. People do feel commitment toward the community; they do have a sense of shared identity and shared moral values. Choices that people make are often inspired by affective and normative motives. Moreover, individuals have only limited intellectual and cognitive capacities, which prevents them from surveying all possible consequences of their actions. Most choices are therefore not rational at all, or only to a limited degree. In short, people are not merely striving for their own pleasure or profits but act also on the basis of internalized values and shared norms. The neoclassical paradigm has not only ignored the moral dimension but has denied its existence.

In the next sections I combine elements from both sociological and anthropological theories relevant to the theme of solidarity, including the functions of ritual for solidarity and cohesion that have not yet been discussed.

Combining Anthropological and Sociological Theory

Reciprocal Obligation

In Mauss's threefold obligation – to give, to receive, and to reciprocate a gift – the principle of reciprocity is succinctly symbolized. As a consequence of these obligations a perpetual cycle of exchanges is set up within and between generations. Social ties are created, sustained, and strengthened by means of gifts. Acts of gift exchange are at the basis of human solidarity. The fact that gifts enhance solidarity is not restricted to the archaic and non-Western societies described by Mauss. In our own society the core meaning of gift giving – its contribution to social ties – has not changed fundamentally, although obviously its role and functions in modern, monetarized society cannot be compared with those in nonmonetarized, archaic society. Whereas in the latter type of society the entire social system, including its economic, legal, religious, and moral foundations, was maintained though gift exchange (it was a "total social phenomenon," as Mauss calls it), in modern society gift exchange has increasingly come to be considered the opposite of economic exchange. Gift exchange is supposed to belong to the private sphere and is associated with informal and not always completely predictable social relations, whereas economic exchange belongs to the domain of the market with its formalized and predictable relations (Brown 1986). Nowadays, gift exchange has become an instance of "social exchange" as opposed to "economic exchange." Gift exchange is supposed to support the "morals" implied in social ties, whereas economic exchange fosters "markets" (Cheal 1988). The differences between social and economic exchange have been summed up by Brown (1986): the terms of social, in contrast to economic, exchange are never explicit and cannot be enforced by law; above all, the definition of equivalency is not discussable.

Although too sharp an opposition between morals and markets has been criticized (see Chapter 1), there remains a difference between the two that relates to their respective potential of bringing about human solidarity: gifts given in informal relationships invariably affect human solidarity, whereas goods exchanged on the market do not. Anthropologists and ethnologists agree on the core role of the moral obligation to return the gift. Because this obligation alternates between the parties involved in exchange, durable social bonds and networks are created enabling patterns of reciprocal exchange to come into existence. Although in sociological theory reciprocal obligation has been recognized as an aspect of solidarity (Weesie, Buskens, and Raub 1998), it has received far less attention in sociology than in anthropology. Nevertheless, the idea of reciprocity is implied in most contemporary conceptions of solidarity and related concepts like trust and cooperation (Misztal 1996).

Motives

The classical sociologists considered solidarity, on the one hand, as based on affective ties and shared norms and values, often associated with the small-scale communities of traditional society; on the other hand, the more instrumental ties of association were supposed to be characteristic of more complex societies where functions are specialized and where market relations have replaced the former subsistence economy. All these authors emphasize that their distinctions between different forms of solidarity are ideal types: in concrete reality the bonds between people often show a certain mixture. The same idea returns in Mauss's essay on the gift: altruism and selfishness are intermingled in the act of giving. It is exactly this mixture that makes gift exchange a self-sustaining system: those who refuse to take part in it place themselves outside the community. In more modern theories on solidarity this important insight has been lost.

In Malinowski's assumption of a continuum of feelings involved in gift giving, the different types of motives underlying solidarity can be recognized: pure gifts, given out of affection, versus barter, a form of exchange that is mainly profit-oriented. Different types of motives in gift giving were thought to belong to different types of social relationships. The idea of a connection between the nature of the feelings involved in gift exchange and the type of social relationship in which it takes place returns in the work of Gouldner and Sahlins. Giving "something for nothing," without any concrete stipulation of returns, is supposed to occur within the circle of close kin, whereas the "attempt to get something for nothing" is more likely with strangers.

In addition to the affection-instrumentality dimension, another significant motive to give and to create social ties comes to the fore, in particular in the work of Simmel, Mauss, Lévi-Strauss, and Gouldner: power. In much anthropological writing the exchange of gifts is analyzed as a contest of honor. This type of gift giving may be seen as a battle revolving around the authority, status, and prestige of the partners involved in the exchange. It is Gouldner's merit to have analyzed the different ways power may be implied in gift exchange. Although we may be inclined to think that equivalence or equality – tit-for-tat – is the main principle of exchange, Gouldner points to the different forms that asymmetrical reciprocity may take. The notion of honor, the dangers of starting and maintaining an exchange process, and the rivalry and power that may color it are regular aspects of gift exchange and of attempts to create social order. Social order comprises not only ties rooted in harmony and peace but power and authority relations as well. The theory of the gift has made this particularly clear.

Equality or equivalence, the idea of quid pro quo, is a common basis of exchange processes as well. To Malinowski the "pure gift" and barter are the more exceptional motives to give, and equality or equivalence is the most common pattern of exchange. Whether equality is in fact the main basis of exchange, more important than, for instance, power, affectivity, or instrumentality, remains a matter of empirical verification, but that it is a regularly occurring pattern has been empirically demonstrated in Chapter 2.

The theory of the gift reveals a range of motives returning in theories of solidarity, but the variety of motives present in gift theory is larger. The various types of motives underlying gift giving correspond to the four models of people's relations to things and to each other, as distinguished by Alan Page Fiske. Whereas sociological theory on solidarity mainly focuses on Fiske's first and fourth type of relationship (affectivity or "community," and instrumentality or "market"), anthropological theories on gift giving demonstrate that, in addition to affectivity and instrumentality, also equality and power may be involved in attempts to create or maintain social order.

Ritual

A final element connecting anthropological and sociological theory on gifts and solidarity is ritual. From Durkheim's sociology of religion (1965 [1912]) – in particular, his analysis of "primitive" Australian cults and beliefs – the enormous impact of ritual for affirming and sustaining social bonds and social structure has become apparent. Religious rituals are adaptive to the life of the community by imposing self-discipline. They bring people together in ceremonies, thereby contributing to solidarity. Ritual also "revitalizes the social heritage of the group and helps transmit its enduring values to future generations" (Coser 1971: 139). Moreover, rituals have a euphoric function by counteracting feelings of frustration and by establishing the sense of being right and acting in a morally justified way.

It is the merit of anthropologists to have uncovered the variety and complexity of the meanings and functions of ritual. They have described and interpreted the numerous rituals surrounding important transitions in the life cycle, or other events that demand sacralization and ritualization (van Gennep 1960; Lévi-Strauss 1966 [1962]; V. Turner 1969; Geertz 1973). In his fascinating account of the Balinese cockfight, Clifford Geertz (1973) offers an interpretation of ritual that differs from the usual functionalist one of reinforcing status positions and social structure. The cockfight can be "read as a text" saying something about Balinese experience. Participating in a cockfight is for the Balinese "a kind of sentimental education" (1973: 449). The ritual symbolizes that society is built of certain emotions like the thrill of risk, the despair of loss, and the pleasure of triumph. "Drawing on almost every level of Balinese experience, it brings together themes – animal savagery, male narcissism, opponent gambling, status rivalry, mass excitement, blood sacrifice – whose main connection is their involvement with rage and the fear of rage, and, binding them into a set of rules which at once contains them and allows them play, builds a symbolic structure in which, over and over again, the reality of their inner affiliation can be intelligibly felt" (Geertz 1973: 449–450). The symbolic structure of the cockfight allows emotions to be expressed while at the same time putting restrictions on them by the setting of rules.

By bringing together assorted experiences of everyday life, the ritual creates a "paradigmatic human event" enabling the Balinese to see a dimension of their own subjectivity that they would not have seen otherwise, at least not in such a condensed form. This seems to be a basic aspect of solidarity as well: by participating in a group activity the individual members learn how to "read" themselves, how their basic emotions become transformed in the interaction with other people, and how their individual being gets shaped through their interdependency with other people. In this sense rituals reinforce the main basis of organic solidarity: mutual dependency. Rituals tie people together because they give expression to feelings of group dependency, even while group members do not share exactly the same values or interpret the ritual in exactly the same way (Kertzer 1988). In addition to the well-known functions of ritual as affirming social ties, revitalizing group life, and promoting the attainment of group goals, at a more basic level it may function as a "school" where lessons can be learned about how the group can contribute to realizing one's own full potential. If it is true, as Durkheim thought, that individuals can only become fully human in and through society, then social rituals presumably fulfill an important socializing role.

In most anthropological work on gift exchange the focus is on the ritual and symbolic aspects of gift giving. Gifts are not primarily or predominantly exchanged for any economic purpose. Rather, they are instruments to convey symbolic messages of the most varied kind, as Lévi-Strauss has argued. Individuals participating in the ritual and respecting its symbols see their "emotional energy" and mutual confidence enhanced. Inversely, persons showing disrespect for the symbols are subject to anger and punishment. The solidarity generated through the interaction processes involved in gift exchange indeed transcends the mere behavioral interaction between the exchange partners by extending it to the emotional mood and the quality of the social relationship.

SIX

❦

Solidarity, Gifts, and Exclusion

A gift that does nothing to enhance solidarity is a contradiction.

(Mary Douglas 1990: vii)

The form of altruism closest to egoism is care of the immediate family. In species after species, we see signs of kin selection: altruism is disproportionally directed at relatives. Humans are no exception.

(Frans de Waal 1996: 212)

Informal gift giving acts as the cement of social relationships because it implies a principle of give-and-take or a norm of reciprocity, as we have seen in the preceding chapters. This is why, according to Mary Douglas (1990), gifts essentially contribute to solidarity. In this chapter we regard a certain type of gift as an expression of solidarity. Gifts can be material as well as nonmaterial. For instance, working as a volunteer for the benefit of the community or providing care or help can be considered gifts. But at the same time these are acts of solidarity toward other people. The degree of directness of the solidarity varies with the social distance involved: from the abstract and anonymous giving to charity, to doing voluntary work for a social organization or for some good cause, to offering concrete help or care to people with whom one is personally involved. As gift giving is more abstract and anonymous, reciprocity will be less. The more familiar one is with the recipient of the gift, the more a form of reciprocity is to be expected. This does not necessarily imply that anonymous gift giving or performing volunteer work is more disinterested than gift giving within the context of personal relationships. As far as empirical data about motives underlying gift giving are available, they show that a range of considerations may be involved, varying from love and affection to self-interested, instrumental, or power-driven motives (see Chapter 2). Although in giving to charitable organizations purely instrumental motives are not very likely, it is not inconceivable that soothing one's conscience or tax deductibility are part of the giver's inspiration.

Just like gifts, solidarity is not always inherently positive in its intentions or consequences. This chapter examines not only positive effects of solidarity but some negative outcomes as well. Within a solidary group pressures toward conformity and egalitarianism may occur. Ingroup solidarity may have negative effects for those who are not participating in the network. Moreover, solidarity may have a selective character in that it promotes the well-being of some but does not contribute to or is even hampering that of others. Initiating ties with some people by means of gift giving implies by definition that others are excluded. Sociologically, it is therefore interesting to investigate which social categories enter into gift relationships and which groups are excluded from these relationships.

This chapter starts by presenting empirical data on some positive manifestations of contemporary solidarity. Three forms of solidarity are examined in detail: giving money, giving time to volunteer work, and giving care or help to persons in one's own surroundings. Data from national Dutch surveys are used to get an impression of the state of solidarity in these respects. The chapter continues with a theoretical discussion of some of the more negative aspects and outcomes of solidarity. In the final section, a selection of data derived from the previously mentioned research project on gift giving in the Netherlands (Komter and Schuyt 1993a; 1993b) is presented in order to demonstrate that solidarity is a two-edged sword: in addition to strengthening human bonds, it may also act as a principle of exclusion.

Positive Manifestations of Solidarity

Giving Money

In the Netherlands large amounts of money are given to charity. During the past ten years there has been a growing "charity market" with a yearly increase in charitable donations. Only about 7% of the Dutch people never contribute to charity. Population growth and the annual rise of net income are some obvious explanations. But also when money gifts are calculated as a fraction of the national income, a slight increase is visible between 1995 and 1999 (T. Schuyt 2001). The Dutch give most to church and ideological organizations (26%), then to health care (17%), international help (16%), environment, nature, animal care (14%), sports and recreation (12%), and societal (10%) organizations. From the work of American authors like Wolfe (1989) and Wuthnow (1991) it appears that the growth of the "third sector" is not an exclusively Dutch phenomenon. Unlike the Netherlands, however, in the United States a decline of money gifts as percentage of the gross national product has been observed (Putnam 2000).

In addition to population growth and income rise, the American sociologist Alan Wolfe (1989) suggests some other factors that might influence people's giving to charity – for instance, trust in the economy and strong family and community ties. The fact that during the past decade the Dutch economy has flourished as almost never before might partly explain the Dutch generosity. Unfortunately, no research is available as yet that is able to clarify the extent to which the increase of donations to charity is caused by population growth, income level, the strength of community ties, the growing number of charities, more aggressive tactics of appealing to people's willingness to donate money, economic developments, the type of welfare state, or the level of state-based social security arrangements (Esping-Andersen 1990).

A recent Dutch report of the Social and Cultural Planning Organisation (SCP 1998) compares the number of members and donors of a range of societal organizations from 1980 to 1996–1997. Although the number of members of religious communities, women's organizations, and political parties has dropped, there is a substantial increase in the sector "international solidarity" (for instance, organizations for medical help, foster parents, Third World help organizations). As these data are based on absolute numbers and as the Dutch population has increased substantially, the picture is not entirely representative. Nevertheless, the authors of the report conclude that these developments in gift giving in combination with the increased membership of ideological organizations (see also the next section) point to a firm sense of citizenship among the Dutch, in our terms, of solidarity.

Giving Time

Volunteer work is generally defined as unpaid work performed within an organized setting to the benefit of other individuals, organizations, or the society at large. Internationally the Netherlands shows up rather well, when it comes to participation in volunteer work. The Social and Cultural Planning Organisation (1998) presents data from 1981 and 1990, comparing volunteer work in twelve countries. In both years the Netherlands occupies a fifth place. In 1990 it comes after the United States, Canada, Sweden, and Norway. Compared with other European countries the number of people participating in volunteer work on a regular basis (and not merely incidentally) is relatively high in the Netherlands, in particular in the domains of culture, recreation, and education.

TABLE 6.1. Volunteer Work in Several Domains for Persons Aged Eighteen and Older, 1977–1995 (weighed outcomes in %)

	1977	1980	1983	1986	1989	1992	1995
Political and ideological aims	4	5	5	5	5	5	7
Occupational, professional, labor organizations	4	6	4	4	4	4	4
Religion, theology	7	11	9	9	10	9	11
Culture, sports, hobbies	17	29	25	25	25	23	27
Education, child nursing, youth work	10	13	15	15	14	13	18
Women	4	6	5	5	4	4	3
Assistance (e.g., advice, information)	4	7	3	2	2	2	4
Help to neighbors, aged, or disabled	11	9	13	11	13	12	14
Number of activities							
None	67	55	59	59	59	61	54
One	23	28	26	25	26	26	28
More than one	10	17	13	11	13	12	14

Source: SCP-Report (1998).

The substantially increased percentage of Dutch citizens as donating members of some organization during the past fifteen years is largely due to their participation in volunteer work. Recreation attracts the largest number of volunteers, but education (parental aid to schools), child nursing, and youth work are also popular. Moreover, since 1977 more time is spent on work with ideological aims. The data, derived from national surveys, are summarized in Table 6.1.

Who are the ones spending their free time to volunteer work? Are there any changes in the number and profile of volunteers during the past fifteen years? About as many people volunteered in 1980 as in 1995, as Table 6.2 shows. About one-third of the Dutch adult population performs some sort of volunteer work. The participation of the younger age group has clearly decreased and constitutes the least active category nowadays, while the participation level of the population aged thirty-five and older has grown. The impact of education has become less: in 1980 the more highly

TABLE 6.2. *Participation in Volunteer Work according to the Time-Allocation Diary by Sex, Age, Education, and Population Category, 1980 and 1995*

	% of Participants		Hours by Participants		% of Leisure Time by Participants	
	1980	1995	1980	1995	1980	1995
All	33	32	4.3	4.9	8.4	8.9
Men	36	31	4.6	6.0	8.9	11.2
Women	29	33	4.0	4.0	7.9	8.0
18–34 years	30	22	4.3	4.5	9.1	9.1
35–54 years	37	39	3.8	5.0	7.9	10.4
55–74 years	33	36	5.2	5.3	8.5	8.5
Lower education	28	27	4.0	4.7	7.3	8.8
Middle education	38	34	4.3	5.3	8.3	10.0
Higher education	47	36	4.9	4.4	10.0	9.0
Four big cities	28	26	4.7	5.1	8.7	9.6
Other 100,000+ cities	34	31	4.7	5.2	8.5	10.4
Rest of the Netherlands	33	33	4.2	4.8	8.3	9.3
(n)	(2,354)	(2,918)	(768)	(933)	(768)	(933)

Source: SCP-Report (1998).

educated formed the most active category, but this is no longer the case in 1995. An interesting gender difference shows up: while men's participation in volunteer work has dropped in 1995 compared with that in 1980, the percentage of participating women has increased. Interestingly, in the same period women's labor participation has also increased substantially in the Netherlands: in 1980 not even one-third of the female population available to the labor market had a paid job, whereas in 1994 this proportion has risen to about half of this population. Although almost half of these are part-time jobs, the total amount of hours women spend in paid work has strongly increased in this period: from 7.2 to 14.6 hours per week. It is therefore striking that women's participation in volunteer work has also increased, particularly the housewives' participation, among whom 41% performs some volunteer work in 1995 against 30%

in 1980. Compared with students, people with or without paid jobs, and retired people, housewives are the most active participants in volunteer work.

Other research (van Daal 1994) offers some more detailed information about the profile of the volunteer. The traditional gender differences show up in the nature of the volunteer work involved, with women spending more time with the sick, elderly, and disabled, with children, and in activities related to school, whereas men spend more of their free time in sports, trade unions, and political organizations. Religious people are, in addition to their work for the church, more active in providing assistance, whereas the more highly educated are relatively well represented in managing functions. What motivates people to spend time in volunteer work? It does not come as a surprise that civic virtues inspired by a concern with all kinds of social issues, humanitarian involvement, and social responsibility are often mentioned as motives. But people also report more instrumental considerations like diversion, seeking social contacts, and entertainment (Willems 1994).

In short, changes in volunteer work over the years do not so much concern the number of people involved because this remains almost constant; rather, it is the profile of the volunteer and the nature of volunteering activities that have undergone changes.

Giving Care

In another report of the Social and Cultural Planning Organisation (1994a) informal care is conceived as an aspect of the broader concept of social support, in particular the instrumental component of it. Informal care comprises practical tasks or concrete services: help with personal or household care. In this study emotional care is not regarded as a part of informal care. The recipients are people who are requiring care according to certain objective criteria that relate to chronic illness or old age. Informal care is considered as having a relatively enduring character: help that

TABLE 6.3. Care Given to Persons Inside and Outside the Household by Persons Aged Sixteen and Older

	Percentage in Sample	Estimated Number of Caregivers in the Netherlands
General care inside the household	20	2,400,000
Care to persons requiring help inside the household	4	500,000
General care outside the household	20	2,400,000
Care to persons requiring help outside the household	10	1,200,000
Care inside and/or outside the household	34	4,100,000
Care to persons requiring help inside and/or outside the household	11	1,300,000

Source: SCP-Report (1994a).

is offered on a regular basis. The care is informal because it is generally given in people's homes and given voluntarily – that is, without financial recompense and outside the context of a professional or organizational setting, like professional assistance or volunteer work. In contrast to professional assistance or volunteer work, informal care is often embedded in a personal relationship between the giver and recipient of the care, as they are participating in the same social network.

In the Netherlands informal care is provided on a large scale. Table 6.3 gives an overview of the amount of care provided inside and outside one's own household, to people who are explicitly requiring care as well as to those who are not. One in three people – about 4 million – are offering help to others in their direct surroundings that is not necessarily related to illness. Table 6.3 also includes general care – that is, caring for relatives living inside or outside one's own household; childcare and household care are excluded. If we look only at care provided to those in need, it becomes apparent that about 1.3 million Dutch people offer this care,

TABLE 6.4. Participation and Time Spent in General Care Inside and Outside the Household by Persons Aged Sixteen and Older, 1975–1990

	Participation (%)				Hours per Week Spent			
	1975	1980	1985	1990	1975	1980	1985	1990
Care inside the household	30	28	22	20	1.4	2.2	1.4	1.6
Care to family members	12	12	12	10	3.5	2.9	3.4	3.8
Care to nonfamily members	14	14	17	12	3.0	3.1	3.7	4.1
Total care outside the household	22	23	26	20	3.7	3.4	4.0	4.5

Source: SCP-Report (1994a).

which amounts to 11% of the population aged sixteen or older. General care is provided by 20% of the population, either inside or outside the household. A quarter of the help provided inside the home is related to illness or disability (0.5 million persons). Half of the care provided outside the home relates to illness (1.2 million of people).

As the individualization process is frequently assumed to have had a negative influence on people's willingness to support one another informally, it is interesting to compare the developments over time. Are there any changes in the contribution to informal care over the years? A comparison of the years 1975–1990 shows that the supply of the care provided outside the home has not undergone any substantial changes (Table 6.4). The proportion of people helping family members remains between 10% and 12%. Somewhat more people, 12% to 17%, offer care to nonrelatives, but again there is no clear trend, although the time spent to care for nonrelatives seems to have increased from 3 to 4 hours weekly. Inside the home the data (in which household and childcare are excluded) show some changes, though: fewer people provide care to relatives (other than their own children) – from 30% in 1975 to 20% in 1990. A possible explanation might be that households have become smaller between 1975 and 1990. The average amount of time spent caring for relatives, however, remains the same – about 1.5 hours weekly.

It is a well-documented fact that the group of informal caregivers consists mostly of nonemployed middle-aged women. The SCP research (1994a) shows that twice as many women as men provide informal care, 15% versus 7%. Most caregivers are between thirty-five and sixty-four years of age. Within the group of informal caregivers 34% of the women are employed as against 61% of the men, while the corresponding figures in the general population are 37% and 64%. Most background characteristics like gender, age, education, and employment have only a very modest influence on whether a person provides informal care. Much more influential is the context in which the care takes place – for instance, the geographical proximity between caregiver and recipient. However, caregivers do display a greater societal concern compared with the population at large: they prove to be more often members of various organizations and are more frequently religious.

As a consequence of the growing number of elderly people and the increase of single persons the demand will inevitably grow. Because SCP prognoses predict that the informal care supply will remain about the same during the next decades, shortages can be expected in the future. For our theme of solidarity, however, it is crucial that on the basis of comparative research over the years no decline in people's willingness to provide informal care is yet visible. That the demand for care will be growing is mainly due to demographic developments in the Netherlands and not to a failing solidarity with fellow citizens.

An important question that remains to be answered is to whom informal care is offered. When do people put aside their own concerns and problems to benefit somebody else? From biological and psychological research on altruism it has become clear that people identify more easily with their near relatives than with others (Wispé 1972; Wilson 1975). Furthermore, identification with those whose interests are congruent with ours is more likely than identification with people unknown to us. Here, an important but largely neglected characteristic of solidarity comes to the fore, namely its selective and excluding nature.

Negative Aspects and Consequences of Solidarity

In sociology solidarity has primarily been conceived as an inherently positive concept. In most theories of solidarity its beneficial effects to the group members are stressed. From the early theories of Tönnies and Durkheim on, it has been assumed that acts of solidarity are directed at achieving a common good and generate feelings of interconnectedness, a "conscience collective," and a shared identity. These theories emphasize the benefits deriving from a *Gemeinschaft* of strong communal ties and shared interests, or from a sound *Gesellschaft* in which mutually dependent individuals profit from a functional division of labor that strengthens their feelings of organically belonging together.

However, solidarity is not predominantly or exclusively the warm and friendly category we usually assume it to be. Various types of risks may be involved in group solidarity (Komter 2001). While several authors have discussed internal risks that threaten solidarity from within the group, its external risks – risks for those who are not participating in the solidary group as a consequence of the behavior of the participating group members – have received far less attention. Internal risks are, for instance, free riding, the decay of the overall salience of solidarity as a consequence of the high costs involved in executing solidarity (Lindenberg 1998), conflicting interests internal to the group (Ostrom 1995), or strong emotional reactions to losses that could result due to the uncooperative behavior of other group members. In strongly tied networks this may lead to vendetta and endless feuds (Uzzi 1997).

Other internal risks to group solidarity are pressures toward conformity and egalitarianism. Strong group norms may impede innovation in organizations. In his discussion on relations of trust, Coleman (1990) mentions as an example the financial community in London. In some financial companies in which trade secrets play an important role there is a general norm against hiring an employee who has left a sensitive position in a competing firm; this group norm may reflect ingroup solidarity, but at the same time the ensuing practice reduces innovation because many good ideas remain unexploited. Although firm groups may successfully mobilize resources in order to maintain themselves, they may at the same time put under restraint the innovating potentialities of individual group members by enforcing conformity to group norms. In addition to harboring tendencies toward conformism, the group may adopt behavioral codes of egalitarianism by sanctioning individuals who perform better or attempt to excel over their fellow group members. Dominant group norms may threaten the individual freedom of the group members by isolating them from the surrounding culture. Among American immigrant communities a person who has aspirations to surpass his or her own group is teasingly called a "wannabe." In their description of what they call a "hyperghetto" Waquant and Wilson (1989) stress the same phenomenon: solidarity based on a common adversity discourages individuals from taking advantage of possible chances outside the ghetto.

What negative external risks may be involved in solidarity? A first example concerns the negative norms and beliefs toward nongroup members. While strong ingroup solidarity favors acting in accordance with the rules of honesty, acceptance of authority, and mutual respect, it may discourage such attitudes toward outsiders. Strong feelings of ingroup favoritism may encourage differential moral standards toward in- and outgroup members: values and behavior of outgroup members are not measured by the ingroup moral standards but are seen as a deviation from these and therefore not as worthy of acceptance or toleration. Groups with strong religious convictions come to mind here (with fundamentalism as an extreme consequence), but also rival football clubs or groups with strongly contrasting cultural backgrounds. Ingroup solidarity may also result in concrete inimical behavior toward outgroup members. The stronger the inclusive power of solidarity, the more pronounced will be the boundaries that separate the ingroup from the outgroup, "us" from "them," and the stronger and more concrete the exclusion of outgroup members will be.

Some attempts have been made to elucidate the relationship between solidarity and exclusion – in particular, those originating in the traditions of economic sociology and anthropology. A representative of the former school of thought, Roger Waldinger (1995), for instance, studied the interaction between economic activity, ethnicity, and solidarity among African American, Caribbean, Korean, and white entrepreneurs in the construction industry in New York. Embeddedness within informal networks of one's own ethnic group engenders social capital promoting people's capacity to obtain scarce resources. Social capital is taken to refer to the advantages ensuing from relationships of mutual trust and cooperation. When somebody has similar ethnic, class, or gender characteristics, he or she is simply perceived as more trustworthy. Mutual trust promotes cooperative behavior and the exchange of information and allows people to profit from their networks (Raub 1997; Raub and Weesie 2000). Waldinger concludes that solidarity has two sides: on the one hand, embeddedness within informal networks fosters economic activity within one's own ethnic community; on the other hand, it is a powerful means to exclude newcomers: solidarity reinforces informal resources for group members but impedes membership for outsiders by refusing them access to these resources. Also Portes and Sensenbrenner (1993) have recognized this phenomenon; they discovered that the same social structures facilitate goal-directed activity for some but put restrictions on the activities of others. The foregoing examples make clear that strong ingroup solidarity may be dysfunctional from the perspective of the wider community: the achievement of the interests of the wider collectivity may be thwarted by the strongly felt ingroup solidarity of its subgroups.

In many cases a combination of internal and external risks occurs, as is shown in de Swaan's (1988) sociological-historical account of the rise of collective state-based solidarity arrangements in various European countries and the United States. From his analysis of the spontaneous associations for mutual financial assistance in case of unemployment formed by Dutch citizens in the nineteenth century, it appears that authentic mutual solidarity was at the same time a strength as well as a weakness of this form of collective care. Although homogeneous membership was a source of solidarity, it could also cause new risks – shortage of expertise, insufficient inspection, no fixed rules and procedures. Moreover, the autonomous collective arrangements resulted in the exclusion of the less privileged citizens.

Strong ingroup solidarity, then, may not only generate pressures toward conformity and egalitarianism, it may also contain the potential for defining other groups as enemies and engaging in conflict with them. Conflict with another group may, in turn, serve to increase the ingroup solidarity of both groups, thereby intensifying the conflict between them (Wrong 1994). More generally, as Georg Simmel (1950 [1908]) already made clear at the beginning of the twentieth century, social ties necessarily imply both bonding and exclusion, namely of those who do not share the distinctive group characteristics and who are allowed neither to share the group aims and interests nor to participate in the activities to achieve these aims and interests. Solidarity and exclusion, then, are two sides of the same coin.

The Two-Edged Sword of Solidarity

That solidarity and exclusion can go together is also illustrated in the empirical results of our study about gift giving in the Netherlands (Komter and Schuyt 1993). In addition to investigating the effects on gift giving of class, gender, and age (see Chapter 2), we studied specific categories of respondents in more detail – retired people, housewives, students, and employed and unemployed people (among whom several respondents were living on disability pensions).

TABLE 6.5. Gifts, Given or Received, according to Social Position, % (N)

	Employed		Unemployed		Retired		Housewife		Student	
	To	From	To	From	To	From	To	From	To	From
Presents	89	66	72	41	77	53	88	75	96	78
	(270)	(200)	(21)	(12)	(46)	(32)	(73)	(62)	(22)	(18)
Money	86	57	55	48	88	22	90	57	61	87
	(261)	(173)	(16)	(14)	(53)	(13)	(75)	(47)	(14)	(20)
Food	72	60	52	52	67	47	71	59	70	74
	(218)	(182)	(15)	(15)	(40)	(28)	(59)	(49)	(16)	(17)
Stay	66	45	55	45	60	30	63	23	87	83
	(200)	(136)	(16)	(13)	(36)	(18)	(52)	(19)	(20)	(19)
Care/help	67	58	55	41	42	40	75	58	78	52
	(176)	(136)	(16)	(12)	(25)	(24)	(62)	(48)	(18)	(12)
(N)	(303)		(29)		(60)		(83)		(23)	

Note: N = 498. The deviation from N = 513 is due to missing participants.
Source: Komter and Schuyt (1993b).

An important precondition to participation in gift exchange is taking part in social networks, circles of friends or family members who meet each other on a more or less regular basis. Many gifts are given during informal meetings between friends (sometimes colleagues) or while having dinner or drinks together. We know by now that much gift giving takes place within still unsettled, yet important social relationships. Our research results confirm this: students appear to be great givers. Other very important occasions of gift giving are the many rituals still surviving in our society. Highlights of ritual gift giving are, of course, Christmas, Valentine's Day, anniversaries, births, wedding ceremonies, jubilees, and the like. Ritual gift giving seems to occur more often within relationships, which have become more or less settled. Women presumably play an important role in ritual giving. Indeed, confirming both Caplow's and Cheal's studies on this point (Chapter 4), the housewives in our sample – together with the students – prove to be the greatest givers, as is shown in Table 6.5.

The Matthew Effect of Gift Giving

Who are the poorest givers and recipients? Table 6.5 shows the results. Unemployed people appear to give less to others than all other categories of respondents, and this holds for all kinds of gifts. The unemployed also appear to receive less than the other respondents on all kinds of gifts, except staying at another person's house. Many authors have pointed to the restricted social networks of people living on minimum wages or on unemployment benefits (Engbersen et al. 1993). Together with their poor financial resources, this might explain the low level of gift exchange among the unemployed. For those living on a retirement pension the same pattern shows up as with the unemployed. With the exception of money gifts, retired people give somewhat less to others, compared with the other categories of respondents. Retired people, however, also receive less than the other categories of all kinds of gifts, except presents; in general, they are the lowest recipients of all categories of respondents.

To summarize: those who give much are also the ones to receive a great deal; this is the positive side of reciprocity. The negative side manifests itself with those categories of people who are not in the position to give much themselves, the (long-term) unemployed and elderly people; they prove to be the lowest recipients. When one's social and material conditions are such that it has become difficult – if not impossible – to give to other people and, related to this, when one has become devoid of social networks, one seems to receive in proportion very little.

Solidarity clearly has a selective character: people seem to choose – probably mostly not in a conscious way – those social partners in their gift relationships who are "attractive" to them, because they can expect them to give in return at some time. The rule of reciprocity tends to disadvantage those who are already in the weakest social position. Merton has called the process of disproportionate accumulation of benefits to those who already have much (in his case academic benefits, like recognition and fame in the academic world) the "Matthew effect," after Saint

TABLE 6.6. *Different Kinds of Help toward the Different Recipients*

	Different Kinds of Help, N (%)[a]					
Recipients	Incidental (moving, small jobs)	Daily Help (transport, gardening, shopping)	Relational (support, comfort, talk)	Childcare	Other	Total Amount
Parents (in-law)	29 (24.8)	64 (54.7)	10 (8.6)	2 (1.7)	12 (10)	117
Own children	20 (54)	5 (13.5)	–	10 (27)	2 (5)	37
Extended family	54 (32.7)	34 (20.6)	23 (13.9)	39 (23.6)	15 (9.1)	165
Friends	53 (37)	21 (14.7)	29 (20.3)	27 (18.9)	13 (9.1)	143
Total amount	156 (33.8)	124 (26.8)	62 (13.4)	78 (16.9)	42 (9.1)	462

[a] Number of times that help was given and percentages of total amount of help given to this category.

Source: Komter and Vollebergh (2002).

Matthew – "... unto every one that hath shall be given" (Merton 1968). The same process applies to gift exchange, as our research demonstrates. Not being able to do good apparently has its own price.

Philanthropic Particularism

Another example of solidarity acting as a principle of exclusion can be deduced from a secondary analysis of the same research data (Komter and Vollebergh 2002). The focus of the analysis was on care as one of the most clear-cut indications of solidary behavior toward other individuals. In particular, we investigated the relative importance of familial solidarity and solidarity toward friends. Therefore, we analyzed which categories of respondents received the most care or help. We identified several kinds of help or care: incidental help, for example, with moving to another place or with odd jobs around the house; help related to daily activities like shopping, gardening, or children's transport; and emotional support, such as offering sympathy or consolation. Table 6.6 shows that most help is given to other family members, then to friends, and finally to parents and children. Note that parents are probably a numerical minority: they consist of at most four people (one's own parents and parents-in-law), whereas the number of other family members and friends may be much greater. Furthermore, Table 6.6 indicates that help and care given to other family members consists of all kinds of help, with a somewhat stronger emphasis on incidental help or care. The same applies to friends. Psychological help is given mostly to family and friends. The percentage given to parents is considerably smaller and appears insignificant where children are concerned: presumably, this kind of help is considered so obvious that respondents do not care to mention it. The same probably applies with giving help to one's partner: this form of help is regarded as so natural that it does not even enter the minds of respondents. For this reason, help or care given to the partner has been omitted from our analysis. This deletion colors our results to some extent; mentioning help or care automatically entails some connotation of obligation: where help is more natural and obvious, the sense of obligation disappears and will no longer be perceived.

Nevertheless, it can be concluded that parents and other family members combined receive more than twice as much help as friends do. Another finding from our research is that people without children give significantly more help and care than people with children, particularly when help and care toward family and friends are concerned (Komter and Vollebergh 2002).

Two conclusions can be drawn from the results. First, parents and other family members combined are overwhelmingly favored over friends when giving care or help is concerned. Second, those with children prove to be less supportive toward their friends and wider family than those without children. Both findings might be interpreted as manifestations of what Salomon (1992) has called "philanthropic particularism," an inherent tendency of voluntary initiatives to favor those with whom one identifies most. Our study demonstrates that solidarity in the form of offering care or help has the same selective character: primary family and extended family taken together do receive more care and help than friends. Those who are deprived of family relationships are clearly at a disadvantage with respect to day-to-day solidarity in the form of care and help.

From our data it can be concluded that the amount of material and non-material gift giving in the Netherlands is substantial and does not warrant any serious worries concerning diminished solidarity or increased self-ishness and individualism: 65% of the respondents reports having given care or help over the past nine months, while 55% has been a recipient of care or help (see Table 2.1). This is the positive side of gift giving. How-ever, the practice of gift giving has a negative side as well. The gift econ-omy appears to possess a rather harsh regularity, which seems to confirm social inequality: those who need it most receive the least. Douglas and Isherwood's observation that "reciprocity in itself is a principle of exclu-sion" (1979: 152) has found empirical substantiation in our research data. People whose social circumstances are deteriorating, for instance, by be-coming unemployed and dependent on state benefits, or by becoming elderly, often face diminishing life chances, shrinking social networks, and increasing isolation. In turn, growing social isolation means less par-ticipation in gift exchange and diminishing opportunities to develop the feelings of "faithfulness and gratitude," as Simmel called them, that are essential in bringing about the wish to return a gift.

The "Matthew effect" causes a substantial imbalance in the distribution of gifts among different social categories, confirming the already existing inequality in social resources. The mechanism of "philanthropic partic-ularism" implies that primarily one's own family benefits from giving care or help. The mechanism may have an evolutionary origin compa-rable with the one underlying altruistic behavior: this behavior proves to be primarily oriented toward relatives and near family (Wilson 1975; Dawkins 1976; de Waal 1996).

As Beck (1986) has argued in *Risk Society: Towards a New Modernity*, the process of individualization leads to winners and losers. Some groups profit from the process by securing themselves a greater autonomy and more options to participate in society. Other groups become separated from traditional support networks and are incurring increasing risks of losing their jobs and incomes. Solidarity as expressed in gift giving appears to have the same two-sided character as individualization: some social categories are clearly benefiting more from it than others. Due to the mechanisms inherent to gift giving that have been described here, solidarity can be considered a two-edged sword (Waldinger 1995).

Inherent Failures of Solidarity

In the Netherlands more and more money is spent on charity. This can partly be explained by the rise in net incomes; however, in combination with the fact that a growing number of Dutch people have become members of ideological (religious and other) organizations, one might as well conclude that there is an increase in civic virtues and solidarity in this respect. Since 1980 the Dutch are active participants in voluntary work, and there have been no signs of decline until now: about one-third of all adults spend some of their time in volunteer work. As concerns informal care, a similar picture arises: the supply of informal care has not changed considerably between 1975 and 1990. Again about one-third of the Dutch provide care to others inside or outside the home.

Although in the common conception of solidarity positive connotations prevail, it is not necessarily a positive concept. Whereas the data from our national surveys do not warrant too pessimistic a view on the level of solidarity as expressed in informal care, our own research on gift giving demonstrates some inherent failures of solidarity. Those people – often the socially weak – who participate less than others in circles of gift exchange are less likely to receive help and care from others than do people who form part of these networks: the "Matthew effect." Moreover, informal care and help are characterized by the restrictions of "philanthropic particularism," a preference to care for family and relatives more than for other people who might require care. Reciprocal solidarity acts as a principle of exclusion in these cases. These inherent failures of solidarity are an important reason why the government can not rely too much on informal care without risking social inequality and exclusion.

∞

In this chapter it has been argued and empirically demonstrated that solidarity may have negative outcomes and consequences in addition to its positive aspects. In public and political debates on social cohesion and solidarity it is often overlooked that solidarity is not merely bonding but also selective and excluding. The ideological and normative uses of the concept of solidarity frequently supersede its analytical use, causing the more negative manifestations of solidarity to disappear from the picture. In the theoretical model to be discussed in Chapter 9, however, these variations of solidarity are included. An important question to be explored in that chapter is under which conditions solidarity is selective: does this mainly apply to the small-scale social units of family and friends, or also to large-scale group solidarity? But first we examine the vicissitudes of family solidarity in more detail. Is it really on the decline, as is feared by many?

∞

SEVEN

Family Solidarity

Given rising divorce rates, it comes as no surprise that people are decreasingly happy with their marriages. . . . Given too, that pleasure in family life is the most important contribution to happiness and life satisfaction, here lies a major explanation of America's current and rising sorrow.

(Robert Lane 2000: 108)

The worst tyrants among human beings . . . are jealous husbands . . ., resentful wives, [and] possessive parents . . . [in] a scene of hatred.

(Peter Laslett 1971: 4)

In most Western countries children and the bonds between generations are still an important source of support for older generations, but concern for the continuity of this support is broadly felt. Over the past two centuries drastic changes have occurred in the nature and extent of family solidarity. Whereas in the absence of social security and institutions of social welfare kin served as the most essential resource for economic assistance and security, a gradual weakening of interdependence among kin has occurred over time. In the past commitment to the survival and economic well-being of the family took priority over individual needs. Also anthropological studies suggest that "kinship dues" were traditionally the main source of kinship support (Sahlins 1972). The instrumental orientation toward family has gradually been replaced by a more individualistic and affective orientation and a greater emphasis on individual needs and personal happiness (Hareven 1995). This development has raised a concern with the vitality of family bonds and intergenerational solidarity. Demographic changes have significantly added to this concern (Bengtson 2001). Never before have elderly people lived so long, and never before has the younger generation been so small in number compared with the older generations. Also the larger variation in family structure is supposed to cause a decline in traditional family patterns and values. International studies about cultural and other values show that the increase of individualization is accompanied by a lower level of identification and loyalty with the family (Inglehart 1977; Popenoe 1988).

In addition to demographic developments changes in the life course may have an impact on family solidarity. Recent research conducted in the Netherlands shows that the phase of childhood and adolescence has become longer in that societal responsibility is postponed (Liefbroer and Dykstra 2000). In adulthood the period in which one participates in paid labor has become shorter. In the Netherlands the percentage of working people aged between fifty-five and sixty-four has decreased from 35% in 1975 to 28.7% in 1998 (*Sociale en culturele verkenningen* 1999). The phase of old age has become prolonged because of the increased longevity. On the one hand, an increasing number of old people will be in need of care and support at a time when the availability of women in particular to provide these has diminished. On the other hand, an increasing number of still vigorous old people will be available to provide support to the younger generation. Both of these developments may affect family solidarity.

Family solidarity is also influenced by the wider social context of the welfare state and its level of social security and caring arrangements. Since their introduction Western welfare regimes incorporate an implicit social contract between generations that is based on intergenerational as well as intragenerational transfers of resources through the mediums of taxation and social expenditure (Bengtson and Achenbaum 1993; Walker

1996; WRR 1999). Public pension provision and the provision of social and health care are the core of this social contract. A similar but informal social contract specifying caring obligations and relationships exists within the family. In both the welfare-state social contract and the implied contract of generations within the family the idea of reciprocity is quintessential. The welfare state has institutionalized the expectation of reciprocity in its system of inter- and intragenerational transfers. Similarly, Bengtson, Rosenthal, and Burton (1990) argue that the contract of generations existing within the family "calls for the parents to invest a major portion of their resources throughout their adult years in the rearing of children; in old age, the care giving is expected to be reversed." Walker (1996) points to the many ways this microsocial contract between family members interacts with the macrosocial one. The economic restructuring of Western welfare states occurring since the 1970s may have profound implications for generational relations within families, particularly when coupled with the increase in life expectancy. Many Western welfare states have faced cuts in social expenditure, thereby putting a higher burden on families to provide informal care. Inversely, the gender-based caring relationship within families is in transition, which may be consequential for welfare-state social policy. The reduction of women's availability as caregivers is a new reality that has to be taken into account in social policy.

This chapter deals with family solidarity, conceived as solidarity within the network of family and near relatives, the informal solidarity contract existing between family members. Precisely because the family is regarded as the breeding ground for Durkheim's mechanical solidarity, it is interesting to examine whether there are concrete indications that family solidarity is declining. First, the theme is positioned within the context of the scientific and societal debate about generations and their interrelationships. Then some theoretical dimensions of intergenerational solidarity are discussed, followed by an overview of empirical research results on concrete intergenerational solidarity in the form of (beliefs about) caring for the elderly by the younger generation. In the final section, a distinction is made between two dimensions of intergenerational relations, the first at the macrolevel of welfare state provisions related to family care, and the second at the microlevel of informal care within the family itself. An interesting question is how both levels interact with one another.

The Relationship between Generations

Relationships between generations have traditionally been a source of great solidarity as well as fierce conflicts. Throughout history members of the younger generation have detested the older generation because of their old-fashioned ideas and beliefs, their rigid attitudes, and their inability to keep pace with the times. The aged, in turn, were faced with a growing emotional distance from the younger generation. Mutual prejudice has always flourished. Contemporary youths do not like reading books anymore, are only interested in watching television or playing computer games, do not feel like making any effort whatsoever, and are materialistic and egocentric. And, in reverse, aged people have had the better opportunities, impede the mobility of the young on the labor market by keeping the better jobs, and reach such elevated ages that they (will) cause an enormous rise of costs in the health care system. These commonsense notions certainly do not offer a satisfying answer to the question whether a serious "generation problem" exists today, as Karl Mannheim termed it in 1928 and, if it does, what its manifestations are.

An important preliminary question is what is exactly considered a generation. Does this concept merely indicate a macrosociological, demographic category based on the year of one's birth? Or is a generation a historical concept, referring to a certain group of people of about the same age, who define themselves as being the founders of new values or the promoters of cultural, political, and social changes, like the Vietnam generation or the baby boomers (Bengtson 1993)? Different views on this matter exist in the scientific literature. Becker (1992), for instance, conceives of a generation as an age cohort occupying a particular position in history and showing similarities at the individual level (life course, values, behavior) as well as the structural level (magnitude, composition, culture, and organization of the generation). When a cohort substitutes for a former one, this substitution process is assumed to be accompanied by a change in values, culture, and life opportunities (Inglehart 1977). The cohort conception of generations has not only been criticized for being static but has an additional disadvantage, which has been termed the "fallacy of cohort-centrism" (White Riley 1992, quoted in Bengtson and Achenbaum 1993): the tendency to assume that all members of one cohort will age in the same way. This assumption precludes the recognition of big differences that may exist within the same cohort, as a consequence not only of differing individual reactions to the aging process but also of the structural influences of, for instance, social class, gender, or ethnicity.

A totally different generation concept has been developed by the founding father of the generation theory, Karl Mannheim (1950 [1928]), who does not so much conceive of a generation as a birth cohort but rather as a group of contemporaries who share the feeling of belonging to a certain generation. This feeling arises as a consequence of shared experiences of particular social and historical events that have been formative for the course of their lives. A birth cohort, therefore, does not necessarily coincide with a generation: rather than age determining a generation, it is the shared conscience. A birth cohort may be at the roots of a generation, but a generation in Mannheim's sense is primarily characterized by a common mutual identification, based on a shared fate that differs fundamentally from that of other generations. This is a much more social-psychological and dynamic view of generations than the statistical and static cohort conception.

For this chapter a mixture of both generation concepts is relevant. Not only age cohorts but also the experience of belonging to a certain generation is important for our theme. One may have grandchildren but at the same time feel "in the midst of life" and be active, for instance, by having a job. A woman may be a grandparent but also be sportive, socially active, and have a circle of friends. Although she belongs to the cohort of the third generation, she feels and behaves as if she were young and is, in that sense, comparable with the members of younger generations. The structure of generations has fundamentally changed during the second half of the twentieth century. More generations have become involved in families. Whereas in former times a family was composed of at most two or three generations due to the shorter life expectancy, nowadays it is not exceptional that four generations are in good health and are contributing somehow to family life. We do not know exactly what the implications of these changes for family solidarity are, but the situation has certainly become different from the one that prevailed during the largest part of the twentieth century when the nuclear family was the main family unit. Everything revolved around father, mother, and the children and, whether you liked it or not, you were dependent on them for your physical and social survival. Even though the nuclear family is still an important anchor and social unit for many people, its importance seems to be diminishing in favor of multigenerational bonds (Bengtson 2001).

Traditionally, the exchange of money, goods, and services has been an important aspect of familial solidarity, in particular as expressed in solidarity between generations. For centuries families have played an important economic role in the lives of individual citizens. Until the era of industrialization the family was the most important unit of production; individual survival depended on economic cooperation within the family. Today economic exchange between family members is no longer a vital precondition for individual survival. Nevertheless, people's well-being still depends largely on the exchange of goods and services with other persons. A substantial part of that exchange continues to occur within the family, among and between generations. In the past two decades, the family is believed to have lost its significance as "a haven in a heartless world" (Lasch 1977). As a consequence of a variety of factors, including women's increased participation in the labor market, their greater economic independence, the liberalization of norms and values, and the increased divorce rate, the family may have lost its former cohesion and original significance. Is there any empirical support for these beliefs?

Family Solidarity: Empirical Research

Dimensions of Family Solidarity

The classical sociologists have left their traces in the literature on intergenerational solidarity. Tönnies's distinction between *Gemeinschaft* and *Gesellschaft* (1987) and Durkheim's theory about mechanical and organic solidarity (1964a [1893]) are based on two elements that have influenced theoretical ideas about intergenerational solidarity: on the one hand, the internalized normative obligations toward the group (mechanical solidarity, *Gemeinschaft*) and, on the other, the functional interdependency of and consensus among group members about the rules of exchange (organic solidarity, *Gesellschaft*; Roberts, Richards, and Bengtson 1991).

The first conceptualizations of family solidarity originated in social psychology. In the 1950s social psychologists started to research group dynamics in the laboratory, especially the characteristics of internal group cohesion. The contribution of Homans (1950), for instance, focused on those elements of human interaction presumed to be determinants of group solidarity. He distinguished between "interaction" or the degree of mutual connectedness of the actions of group members (Durkheim's functional dependency), "extendedness" of group activities, degree of mutual affection, and norms concerning group membership and activities. The greater the interaction, mutual affection, and shared norms and commitment to the group, the more cohesion the group would show. Another social psychologist, Heider (1958), added the degree of resemblance among group members to the factors listed by Homans. In addition to having frequent contact, also shared interests and norms contribute to group cohesion.

These contributions are reflected in the work of the contemporary American family sociologist Bengtson. In a recent article (2001) he summarizes the solidarity model developed by him and his colleagues (Bengtson and Mangen 1988; Bengtson and Roberts 1991; Roberts et al. 1991). The model consists of six dimensions of intergenerational solidarity: affectual solidarity (how people feel about their relationships), associational solidarity (type and frequency of contact), consensual solidarity (agreement in opinions and values), functional solidarity (assistance), normative solidarity (expectations regarding family obligations, familistic values), and structural solidarity (opportunity structure for interaction, geographical proximity). Using longitudinal data, Bengtson and his colleagues have been able to chart the course of intergenerational solidarity over time. Between 1971 and 1997 they found remarkably stable patterns of affectual solidarity in the United States: high levels of emotional bonding across generations have remained intact over the years, according to Bengtson.

Bengtson's typology of solidarity dimensions has given rise to extensive empirical research. One of the questions posed by researchers concerns the relationship between the dimensions of solidarity. Despite the original hopes of detecting one underlying construct of solidarity, only associational, functional, and structural solidarity show substantial intercorrelation, and these dimensions, in turn, prove unrelated to affectional solidarity. In the absence of a theoretical model specifying the causal relationships between the concept of family solidarity and its indicators, each dimension has been studied separately. In their overview of empirical research Roberts et al. (1991) mention, among others, the following results. Normative intergenerational solidarity has been found to be stronger when parental income is lower. Affectional solidarity is related to age and gender and is stronger among members of older generations and women (mothers and daughters). Associational solidarity has also been found to be higher among women, probably reflecting their "kinkeeping" role. Among divorced parents, as well as among people living in an urban setting and those with higher education, associational solidarity seems to be lower. Probably because functional solidarity or the exchange of help and care is relatively easy to study empirically, studies assessing the conditions under which assistance flows both up and down generational lines in the family are abundant (Cheal 1983; Mangen et al. 1988; Roberts et al. 1991). Functional solidarity appears to be positively correlated with higher income and education and with marital status.

There are several problems connected to Bengtson's typology. For instance, some of the dimensions, in particular associational and functional solidarity, seem to be partly overlapping; helping a family member necessarily means having contact and seeing him or her. Second, no attempt is made to develop a theoretical model in which the causal relationships between the dimensions and the putative construct of family solidarity are specified. In Bengtson's view family solidarity seems to be the sum of the dimensions, which implies a certain level of internal consistency between them. Empirical research has not confirmed this, though. Moreover, the nature of the causal relationships between the dimensions themselves is not clear. Geographical proximity (structural solidarity) is clearly a constraining (or enabling) factor where associational and functional solidarity are concerned and, in that sense, is at a different causal level. A third problem is that none of the dimensions has been studied in any depth, so that no progress is made to arrive at a better theoretical understanding of the complex and multifaceted concept of family solidarity. A study done by the American sociologists Alice and Peter Rossi (1990), however, has attempted to investigate these aspects of family solidarity in greater detail.

The Nature of Family Ties

The Rossis made use of Bengtson's dimensions of family solidarity in a study of 323 parents and 287 adult children. Focusing their analysis on associational, functional, affectional, and consensual solidarity they found substantial correlations between contact frequency (associational solidarity) and help exchange (functional solidarity). Also, a relationship between value consensus (consensual solidarity) and affective closeness (affectional solidarity) showed up. A lack of connection was found between contact frequency and value consensus. Apparently, some degree of interaction is socially expected and occurs regardless of a consensus about core values among parents and children. Neither was there a substantial relationship between help exchange and value consensus; help exchange occurs independently of the subjective feelings of children and parents toward each other.

The Rossis' research demonstrates that only two sets of the dimensions of family solidarity as distinguished by Bengtson show consistent and substantial correlations: functional solidarity (help exchange) and associational solidarity (contact frequency), and consensual (value consensus) and affectional solidarity (affective closeness). That connections are found between help exchange and contact frequency is somewhat of a tautology, as was said earlier. Also the relationship between shared values and mutual affection does not come as a surprise, because having similar ideas on religious and political matters is an important (though not necessarily the only or the most important) precondition to mutual liking and emotional closeness.

The main motivational base for providing assistance to parents or adult children seems to be internalized norms of obligation. That is probably the reason why the Rossis devote two chapters of their book to this issue. The structure of these norms appears to be systematically patterned: not the type of the kin person but the degree of relatedness of ego to the various kin types was what mattered most. Children and parents take priority over all other kin; siblings are the next in the hierarchy of felt obligations, followed by grandchildren and grandparents. Still less obligation was felt to nieces, nephews, aunts, and uncles.

As to the affectivity dimension the Rossis report evidence of the continuing effects of early family experiences on current relations between parents and adult children. Similar characteristics were transmitted from one generation to the next. For instance, the quality of the parents' marriage was echoed in the marital happiness of adult children. A more global quality of family life – family cohesion – was also transmitted cross-generationally: happy, cooperative, interesting families tended to breed families with similar characteristics themselves. Gender remains a very significant factor in family life. Women keep playing a central role, not only in the organization of the household and in child rearing but also in the emotional climate of the family. Value consensus had an important impact on the affective tone of parent-child relations. Dissensus in core values (religion, politics, general outlook on life) depressed the emotional closeness of parents and adult children.

As regards the next dimension, social interaction, the Rossis conclude that their respondents had widespread access to both their own parents and to their adult children. Apparently adult children did not move far away from their parents in most cases. The access profile is reflected in the contact between generations: from a third to almost half of the adult children saw a parent at least once a week; one in five adult daughters had daily phone contact with her mother. Most respondents were satisfied with this contact frequency and, if they were not, they overwhelmingly preferred more rather than less contact (often because one feels one "should" have more contact). Whereas distance represented the major factor affecting the frequency of interaction between mothers and adult children, the quality of the relationship with fathers was even more of an influence than sheer opportunity. Family size, in particular of the parental generation (the number of children the parents had) but also of the younger generation (the number of their own children), reduced social interaction between individual members of different generations.

Accessibility of the generations (Bengtson's "structural solidarity") is, of course, the fundament for both interaction and help exchange. Gender differences were found, not only in social interaction but also in help exchange. More women than men had regular contact with their parents, and the help exchanged between the generations was most extensive in the mother-daughter relationship. The quality of the emotional bond between parent and child in the past had continuing direct effects on the frequency of contact and the amount of help exchanged. The help parents gave to children tended to be more instrumental (advice, job leads, money), whereas the help children gave to parents was more personal, hands-on care giving. Income had a strong impact on help between generations: the higher the income of parents, the more extensive was the help they gave to adult children. The exchange of help varied according to the stage of the life course. Much help was given to young adults; as the young adults matured, this help diminished, whereas children kept giving support to their parents. As parents grew older they received more support, particularly from their daughters. Apparently there is a decline in the reciprocity in the exchange of support between generations over the course of life.

Intergenerational Solidarity: Values and Beliefs

Which beliefs exist on the obligations of the younger to the older generations when the latter are in need of care and help? The Euro-barometer surveys on public beliefs about elderly people provide a good international overview (Walker 1996). One question posed in these surveys concerns the extent to which one agrees with the statement that working people are obliged to contribute to a decent living standard for elderly people by means of paying taxes or other financial contributions. Walker (1996), who interprets the answers to these questions in terms of solidarity, concludes that there is a remarkably high level of solidarity; a strong agreement with the statement is found among 60.1% of the Danes, 45.9% of the British, 45.7% of the Spanish, 42.4% of the Dutch, 41.2% of the Portuguese, and 40.7% of the Irish. Somewhat lower percentages are

TABLE 7.1. Beliefs about Solidarity of the Young with the Aged, 1997 (% agreeing)

	18–44	45–64	65–79
If the costs of retirement pensions rise, older people should pay more taxes.	17	20	20
If the costs of the health care system keep rising, older people should pay their own contribution.	66	49	40
If insufficient jobs are available, older and younger people are equally entitled to have one.	81	77	72
If the number of older people requiring help increases, particularly the young should provide more care.	59	56	67

Source: Dykstra (1998).

found in Greece, Italy, Luxembourg, Belgium, and Germany, with the lowest percentage of 25.9% found in France (Walker 1996).

In the Netherlands the Dutch Demographical Institute (NIDI) has investigated beliefs about assistance for elderly people requiring care (Dykstra 1998). A large majority, 93%, thinks that the government has the prime responsibility when caring provisions for elderly people in need of physical or financial assistance are concerned. Another 65% are of the opinion that aged people should, in the first place, appeal to the government when they need care and only afterward ask their children for help if necessary. Table 7.1 presents an overview of beliefs about solidarity of the young for the aged.

A minority of both the younger (17%) and the older age groups thinks that in case of rising costs of the pension system, the elderly should start paying more taxes. However, younger people do think that the elderly should assume some financial responsibility for the rising costs of the health care system. When asked for their opinion about being entitled to a job in times of economic scarcity, more of the younger than of the older age group think that both young and old are as much entitled. Also a relatively large number of young people, 59%, are willing to assume some responsibility for elderly people requiring care.

Caring for Family

What people think or believe does not always correspond to how they actually behave. It is much easier to say that one feels solidarity toward older people than it is to behave according to that feeling. What picture arises when we look at concrete care and support provided to older people? How do the recipients of the care experience that support and which motives are underlying the behavior of the caregivers?

Figures of the European Community Household Panel of 1994 show that adult children, particularly women, provide a large share of the informal care given to older generations (Dykstra 1997). About 10% of all European adults between thirty-five and sixty-four years of age provide unpaid care to members of older generations on a daily basis, about 14% of women versus 6% of men. In the Netherlands about 13% of all adult women, in particular those between forty-five and fifty-four, provide informal care to aged people, an ample half of them spending more than four hours daily.

Dykstra and de Jong-Gierveld (1997) have examined the conditions under which parents receive support from their children, using a sample of 1,122 Dutch men and women between fifty-five and eighty-nine, who required care. A distinction between informal and formal care was made, and people with and without a partner as well as divorced or widowed people were included in the sample. The results are shown in Table 7.2.

Aged people with a partner are in the first place receiving help from their partners. With respect to intergenerational solidarity it is interesting to observe that 15% to 20% of the aged people who still have a partner receive help from their children. Children apparently are the second source of help but, for people who need help and do not have a partner, they are the first source to rely on. This applies much more strongly to people whose partner has died than to divorced people. Apparently, a divorce may have long-term consequences for the relationship with children. It is far less self-evident for children of divorced parents to provide informal care

TABLE 7.2. Sources of Help for Men and Women Aged Fifty-five and Older, Having Children, and Requiring Daily Practical Help (%)

	First Marriage		Ever Widowed		Ever Divorced	
	M	F	M	F	M	F
With (marital) partner, receives *informal* care from						
Partner	63	63	54	—[a]	47	73
Other members of the household	5	5	3	—[a]	3	12
Children living outside the home	25	25	23	—[a]	0	15
Other family members	4	3	6	—[a]	3	0
With (marital) partner, receives *formal* care	18	26	20	—[a]	18	42
Without (marital) partner, receives *informal* care from						
Members of the household	—[a]	—[a]	8	7	0	3
Children living outside the home	—[a]	—[a]	47	53	13	23
Other family members	—[a]	—[a]	6	11	0	10
Without (marital) partner, receives *formal* care	—[a]	—[a]	54	50	50	46

[a] Too few cases.

Source: Dykstra and de Jong-Gierveld (1997).

and help than it is for children whose parents are still married. Divorced fathers, of all categories, receive the least support from their children. On the other hand, children from a possible second marriage have a more important share in caring for their once divorced fathers than is the case for their divorced mothers. As to the relationship between informal and formal care, Dykstra and de Jong-Gierveld (1997) conclude that those who receive little informal care do not seem to appeal for formal care more frequently. On the contrary, the most frequent users of informal resources are at the same time using formal resources to the largest extent.

Several investigations suggest a relationship between social class and intergenerational solidarity. Kulis (1992), for instance, points to certain common ideas with respect to solidarity and social class: it is often thought that lower-class people offer each other mainly practical and instrumental help, whereas the middle and higher social strata would more often exchange emotional and financial support. In a large-scale survey Kulis distinguished between instrumental, economic, and social help. He found that, contrary to existing beliefs, middle-class parents offered more instrumental help to their children than lower-class parents did; the same applied to financial and social-emotional help. From a secondary analysis of the data of the Dutch research into gift giving already mentioned in earlier chapters, a class-bound difference in gift-giving patterns appeared to exist between a "friends culture" and a "family culture." More highly educated people appeared to give more to friends, whereas the lesser-educated gave mainly to family. This was the case for all kinds of gifts, material as well as nonmaterial, including care and help (Komter and Vollebergh 1997).

Finally, it is important to pay some attention to family solidarity in the context of the immigration society that many Western European countries have become over the past decades. In their research among legal and illegal immigrants in the Netherlands, Engbersen and Burgers demonstrate substantial patterns of mutual care and help (Komter, Burgers, and Engbersen 2000). A special form of family solidarity among members of minority groups is the continuous financial support in the form of regular remittances provided to family members who have remained in their native country. In times that are increasingly characterized by immigrants' transnational activities and border-crossing ties and loyalties (Snel and Engbersen 2002), it can be expected that transnational forms of family solidarity will increase rather than diminish.

The Troubled Side of Family Solidarity

An interesting finding is that a high level of intergenerational solidarity does not necessarily coincide with the psychological well-being of aged family members (Mutran and Reitzes 1984) and in some cases may even threaten it (Roberts, Richards, and Bengtson 1991). Under certain conditions, such as strong financial pressures, high family solidarity generates mental tension caused by obligations that are too much and too heavy and by too strong an appeal to one's time and resources. In a small-scale qualitative investigation among older men and women in London, Gail Wilson (1993) found also that intergenerational solidarity is not self-evidently experienced as something positive. Often there is a lack of reciprocity (old age restricts the possibility to return help and care), causing feelings of dependency. Receiving and accepting help and care is not without problems in this case. Moreover, the care may be experienced as a form of control – is the house kept clean enough, does one eat regular meals? Many young people experience the care they provide to their aged parents as a burden. Several aged respondents from Wilson's research remarked that when the young offer a lot of help, "love declines and duty takes over" (1993: 639). Also Janet Finch argues in her book *Family Obligations and Social Change* (1989) that women's motives to care for their aged family members may be rooted in a form of "prescribed altruism," a strongly felt inner norm of being obliged to demonstrate solidarity with aged family members. These inner obligations to intergenerational solidarity are, of course, strongly connected to the gendered division of labor and care that still survives in our society.

Various studies on aging and the family discuss the possible negative consequences of intergenerational solidarity, the ways the caregiver's psychological well-being may be threatened (Ryff and Seltzer 1995, 1996), or the impact stressful events may have on the quality of parent-child relations (Suitor et al. 1995). Family support can become troubled by conflictive aspects of relationships (House, Umberson, and Landis 1988; Bengtson 2001). People may control their relatives or express all kinds of relational demands, thereby burdening the relationship. As Boszormenyi-Nagy and Spark have argued convincingly (1973), feelings of loyalty, solidarity, and mutual trust are dependent upon the silent bookkeeping of giving and receiving among family members. This silent bookkeeping may be transmitted from one generation to the next. Parents try to make up for shortcomings in their own upbringing by giving their children what they missed themselves; children again compensate for the imperfections they experienced. In reality family ties are often a mixture of (longings for) love and disappointment or anger, feelings of dependency, and a desire for autonomy – in short, they are essentially ambivalent (Luescher and Pillemer 1998). Troubled or ambivalent feelings underlying family ties may be an important cause of a later lack of solidarity, or of a solidarity characterized by insincerity, insecurity, and stress.

In the Netherlands Ali de Regt (1993) has signaled the sense of obligation that many young people feel toward their parents. Often these feelings are aroused when paying their parents a visit, or helping them in case of illness. As a consequence of their increased financial resources parents nowadays are caring for their children during a much longer period than was the case in the past when children went out to work at a much younger age. Formerly existing expectations of children caring for the physical and material well-being of their parents have become less compelling, but the new financial dependency of children may contribute to their feeling obliged toward their parents. Although affection will in many cases be involved in the relationship between parents and their young adult children, these feelings are not self-evident (they perhaps never were) and will often be mixed up with forms of "prescribed altruism."

There are some empirical indications of a gender difference in caring motives: daughters would be more often driven by altruistic motives whereas among sons feelings of obligation, expectations concerning inheritance, and the frequency of existing contacts would prevail (Dykstra and de Jong-Gierveld 1997). More generally, feelings and motives prove to be strongly related to the category to whom help and care are provided: feelings of moral obligation are predominant when help is given to family but help to friends is more often accompanied by feelings of affection, regardless of gender (Komter and Vollebergh 1997).

The evidence suggests that the existing concern about the level of contemporary family solidarity is not justified: neither in the United States nor in certain European countries has a significant decline in the level of help and care provided by adult children to their parents been observed, and people's beliefs reveal a clear awareness of their own obligations toward the older generation. Small-scale, in-depth studies such as Wilson's are still scarce, but it is exactly this type of study that could shed light on the more problematic aspects of family solidarity (Johnson 2000). In distinguishing the motives for caring for family members, there seems to be a subtle balance between reciprocity, affection, and obligation.

Macro- and Microsolidarity

Most welfare states are based on a silent contract between generations, with the younger generation contributing financially to the care needed by the elderly (Walker 1996). Through the payment of taxes and premiums and by means of social policy, the government provides for the material and physical support required by aged people when they are not able anymore to earn their own living or to care for themselves properly. Western and Northern European countries have a relatively generous system of pensions and additional forms of (partly) subsidized governmental support for the elderly compared with the United States – home care, district nursing, adaptations to the homes of the disabled, meals delivered at home, to mention a few examples. In view of this situation it is not surprising that many aged people living in Western and Northern Europe prefer the institutional, state-provided care over an enduring dependency on their own children (de Jong-Gierveld and van Solinge 1995).

The micro- and macrosocial dimensions of intergenerational relations are not completely separate phenomena; in fact, they are interdependent in several ways. First, characteristics of welfare-state social policy for aged people – in particular, the liberality and accessibility of caring arrangements – have an impact on care provision within families. For instance, cuts in governmental elderly care may cause a stronger appeal to informal caregivers, implying a higher workload for them. Similarly, changes in the level of the pensions may have an impact on the financial and physical dependency of aged people upon their family members. These developments are often unintended side effects of governmental policy. A second influence of the state upon microsocial, intrafamilial caring arrangements is the social construction and embodiment of traditional family ideals in which women are still playing an important role as informal caregivers. In many Western countries governments are hesitant to intervene in too direct a way into the caring potential of families because they fear that an overly generous governmental supply of care will eliminate spontaneous care provided within families (Walker 1996). A paradoxical effect becomes visible here: whereas the traditional family ideal is declining rapidly, the principle of governmental nonintervention acts as a reinforcement of traditional family relationships.

But the influence also goes the other way around: microsocial arrangements are reflected in macrosocial policy, or in the use that is made of macrosocial arrangements (Esping-Andersen 1999). The nature and quality of the relationship between parents and their adult children may have an impact on the willingness of the children to provide care to their parents and, therefore, on the extent of the appeal that is done to formal caring arrangements. Also the extent to which adult children and their parents have access to formal, state-based arrangements and facilities will influence the balance between formal and informal care within a particular family. Financial resources as well as knowledge of formal opportunities to obtain the necessary care and support are some obvious determinants of the actual use that is made of public benefits.

What, then, is the nature of the relationship between the macro- and the microsocial contract between generations? The idea that a decrease of caring provisions by the welfare state will lead to an increase of informal care has been propagated by politicians at a time when European welfare states are being economically restructured: family care as a substitute for state-based care. The substitution thesis may also work the other way around and is often expressed as a fear: the more the state cares for its citizens, the fewer citizens will care for each other. An alternative way to understand the relationship between the macro- and the microsocial dimensions of intergenerational relations is the complementarity thesis, which holds that higher levels of formal care go together with higher levels of informal care.

Empirical research done so far offers a varied picture: in some welfare states the substitution thesis is confirmed, whereas in others the complementarity thesis seems to hold (Knijn and Komter 2003). A straightforward answer to the question of which thesis is the most valid in general is not to be expected. The reason is that the nature of the relationship between the macro- and microsocial contract seems to depend on the liberality of the particular welfare state and of the specific domain that is studied (childcare, informal care, intergenerational transfers, etc.).

In the Netherlands several empirical studies corroborate the complementarity thesis (Komter et al. 2000). For instance, the findings of the previously mentioned study by Dykstra and de Jong-Gierveld (1997) demonstrate that the most frequent users of informal resources are also using formal resources to the largest extent. The main focus of the recent book by Arber and Attias-Donfut (2000) is the exchange of material and nonmaterial support between adult generations within a framework of the interaction between the public and private domains. They report a German study by Künemund and Rein (1999) who used data from a large comparative survey of older people in four Western countries and Japan. The study shows that "the most important forms of solidarity with regard to older people take place in those countries where social policies are generous to the welfare of older people" (Arber and Attias-Donfut 2000: 13). These findings confirm the notion that public aid reinforces private aid rather than substituting for it. Other research results reported by Attias-Donfut and Arber also show that the rise in public caring provisions during the past decades has not resulted in any reduction of informal care within families. From their own study on three-generational families in France, based on a representative sample of multigenerational families, the same picture arises. The authors conclude: "The complementarity of public and private forms of support has been shown for different categories of transfers. Whether these transfers are for financial help for young adults or care given to the eldest-generation members, the results are the same. In all cases, public benefits increase the recipient's chances of an additional and complementary form of support from members of their family lineage" (Arber and Attias-Donfut 2000: 65). In short, public transfers reshape and sustain family solidarity (Kohli 1999).

Family Solidarity: Solid but Ambivalent

Beliefs about extrafamilial, state-based intergenerational solidarity generally show a high level of solidarity. In the Netherlands as well as in many other European countries, there is a high consensus about the desirability of working people's financial contribution, through taxes or otherwise, to a decent standard of living for aged people. The Dutch grant a very important role to the government when it comes to provisions for elderly people requiring care or help. The majority of the Dutch think that the government is primarily responsible for elderly care and that children's role is only secondary. In daily reality, however, children still provide informal care to older family members to a substantial extent. The Dutch level of informal care provided by adult children, particularly women, to older generations is no exception to the levels found in other European countries. Despite fears to the contrary, the state of actual family solidarity in the Western world is still very solid.

Although family care is still provided on a large scale, the motives underlying the care offered to aged (in-law) parents are based on inner obligation – a kind of "prescribed altruism" – rather than on feelings of affectivity and identification. Recipients may experience the care offered to them as problematic. For instance, the parents' psychological well-being may not be served best when their own children are the caregivers.

The care and help may be felt as a form of control, and the diminished reciprocity when the recipient is older may cause feelings of dependency. Inversely, caregivers frequently experience the care as a heavy burden in terms of the time and the resources they spend on it.

Whereas the concept of family solidarity seems to direct our attention automatically to positive feelings of connectedness and altruistic acts of helping, we should bear in mind that the nature of family ties is fundamentally different from that of other social ties in that they are given, not chosen. Family solidarity cannot be isolated from the more negative aspects of care provided to family and from the deeply ambivalent nature of family ties in general. On the one hand, the bonds between family members are still solid in terms of the amounts of care and help that continue to be exchanged; on the other hand, family ties may be troubled or conflictive and be experienced as a burden.

PART III

Contemporary Solidarity

EIGHT

∾

Changing Solidarity

> In some areas of our public life a shared sense of civility seems to have been *delegitimated* as a binding norm we can reliably invoke; that is, not merely that people behave uncivilly, but that the charge "That was uncivil" carries little or no weight. So I think there is a decline in civility and that this decline *matters*.
>
> (Lawrence Cahoone 2000b: 145)

Contemporary solidarity is different from what it has been in earlier times. Broad societal changes have had an impact on the forms and manifestations of solidarity: the individualization process, the decline of religiosity in Western societies, the economic reforms that have taken place in many welfare states, changing patterns in family life, changing gender roles, the development of the information and communication technology, and, last but not least, the migration processes occurring throughout the world. As a consequence of immigration new religious and political identities present themselves to the inhabitants of the Western world, giving rise to new questions and concerns about solidarity. These societal changes do not necessarily cause a decline in solidarity, as is often assumed. In certain domains solidarity may increase; in others it may merely adopt a new shape. In this chapter, I briefly examine some of the main dimensions that may be involved in the transformation in solidarity: individualization, diversification, and globalization. Mainly cultural critics have reflected on these societal transformations, but their conclusions only incidentally extend to the consequences for social ties and solidarity. This is understandable because it is almost impossible to connect broad societal changes causally to changes in solidarity. The societal changes are too complex and solidarity is too multifarious to allow clear causal statements. In the second part of this chapter I address some changes in contemporary solidarity and, where possible, support these with empirical data.

A first and overriding societal change is the individualization process. This development has its starting point in the nineteenth century (although its roots go back to a more distant past) and has been reflected on by classical sociologists like Durkheim and Simmel. In their view one of the consequences of individualization is that solidarity would become more abstract. With the modernization of society people would come to participate in an ever larger number of partly overlapping social circles. This would enlarge their individual possibilities to choose; loosen the former tightly knit ties of family, neighborhood, and church; and weaken the formerly existing solidarity patterns.

A second and related development is diversification: of identities, preferences, convictions, and commitments. It is assumed that the former continuity and stability of human identity are disappearing, and that the sharing of beliefs, roots, or traditions with fellow human beings is becoming less self-evident. Although modern individuals are more capable than ever to assert their own selves, they are at the same time experiencing a growing insecurity about what is going on in society, socially, culturally, and materially. The presence of an increasing number of "strangers" in modern Western societies adds substantially to this uncertainty. Hospitality toward strangers, once a moral obligation and a daily practice all over the world, has lost its former meaning as an expression of solidarity.

The third change concerns the globalization process, the widening of political, economic, technological, social, and cultural borders allowing for worldwide interconnections between organizations and people that create new possibilities and exigencies for solidarity. One manifestation of this development is the new communication technology, in particular the Internet, which creates new networks between millions of people.

Changing Society, Changing Individuals

Individualization and Social Ties

The individualization process has emancipated humans from the web of mutual dependencies existing within the traditional community. The individual has been freed from the ascribed, inherited, and inborn determination of his or her social standing, which is now ruled by self-determination. Choice and change of identities have replaced the former determination. Growing autonomy and freedom have resulted from the individualization process, but there is another aspect as well. In the words of the indefatigable commentator of postmodernity, Zygmunt Bauman, "the other side of individualization seems to be the corrosion and slow disintegration of citizenship" (2001: 49; see also 1997, 1998). Individuals tend to be skeptical of the common good or the "good society," and individual troubles do not easily add up to a common cause anymore.

In Bauman's view modern individuals are increasingly selfish, cynical, and indifferent to long-term life projects. He perceives signs of an overwhelming feeling of disorientation and loss of control over the present world, resulting in a fading of political determination and a disbelief in the effectivity of collective or solidary action. In Western Europe one can indeed observe an increasing dissatisfaction with the welfare state and politics as such. The institutions of the welfare state are the object of growing resentment. The traditional efforts of the welfare state – providing support to those who, for whatever reason, are not able to support themselves – are sensed as "normal," and the millions of people who, thanks to these provisions, are able to live a decent life are not heard about. As welfare has transformed into being a right instead of a favor, people seem to have lost their interest in the welfare state. At the same time in many countries a substantial resentment about the political ineffi- cacy can be observed; in the Netherlands the main concerns are health care, education, and public transport. This resentment, however, is not an exclusively Dutch phenomenon but is broadly felt in other Western European countries as well (Misztal 2001).

Various commentators have pointed to a decline of people's involve- ment in long-term commitments, whether in work or with other people. Social bonds and partnerships would be increasingly regarded as things to be consumed, not produced. Bauman, for instance, observes rather gloomily that the human bond "is not something to be worked out through protracted effort and occasional sacrifice, but something which one expects to bring satisfaction right away, something that one rejects if it does not do that and keeps and uses only as long as (and no longer than) it continues to gratify" (Bauman 2001: 157).

In the same vein Beck (1986) argues that in our individualized society contemporary social relations are subject to high risk and are therefore facing high levels of uncertainty. The nuclear family as the last form of synthesis between generations and genders has disintegrated, and indi- viduals have become increasingly burdened with the responsibility for their own fate. The individualization process has resulted in a growing confusion over the stability and duration of marriage. The result for the individualized citizens is that their life patterns and careers are increas- ingly fragmented.

Another cultural critic, Richard Sennett, describes in his book *The Corrosion of Character* (1998) how radical changes in the way work is organized have influenced the individual's sense of identity and experi- ence of self. Whereas in the past the world of work was hierarchical and rigid, nowadays it has become less embedded in hierarchical relations and more flexible. Whereas the former work ethic asserted the self-disciplined use of one's time and the value of delayed gratification, the contempo- rary organization of work requires short-term teamwork, adaptability to circumstances, and risk taking. As a consequence contemporary citizen's ability to develop a sense of sustained purpose and longer-term commitments would be threatened. In Sennett's view the new economic order and the way work is organized are undermining interdependency – one of the main conditions for the coming into being of social bonds. The organizational structure of large-scale institutions obliterates the mutual dependency and reciprocity among those involved. The anonymity and bureaucracy of these organizations diminish the sense of mattering as a person, whereas it is only in direct interaction with others that people can feel they are needed. Feeling superfluous may lead to a lack of responsiveness and mutual trust and is thereby a potential threat to solidarity, according to Sennett.

The picture arising from the views of these cultural critics – from both the United States and Europe – is that in the new society feelings of being rooted to a certain place or of being bound together by collective interests have diminished and, in many cases, even got lost. People's capacity to initiate relations of trust have decreased, whereas at the same time trust is seen as an important condition for solidarity (Misztal 1996; Putnam 2000). Within organizations the mutual dependency between individuals has diminished. Institutions that formerly were capable of binding people together, such as the family, the neighborhood, religion, or the nation-state are in decline (Turner and Rojek 2001). Social ties have lost their predictability and have become more transitory.

The Assertive Self

Solidarity is not merely based on mutual dependency and the capacity to trust other people but on a more fundamental capacity as well: the capacity of putting oneself in the imaginary position of the other. Long before George Herbert Mead (1961 [1934]) formulated his theory of the development of the inherently social nature of the self – the self as the mirror of other people's beliefs and attitudes – Adam Smith, in his book

The Theory of Moral Sentiments (2002 [1759]), offered a similar account of the way in which we learn to judge our own conduct and sentiments: by comparing our behavior with that of other people.

The principle by which we naturally either approve or disapprove of our own conduct, seems to be altogether the same with that by which we exercise the like judgments concerning the conduct of other people. We either approve or disapprove of the conduct of another man according as we feel that, when we bring his case home to ourselves, we either can or cannot sympathize with the sentiments and motives, which directed it. And, in the same manner, we either approve or disapprove of our own conduct, according as we feel that, when we place ourselves in the situation of another man, and view it, as it were, with his eyes and from his station, we either can or cannot entirely enter into and sympathize with the sentiments and motives which influenced it. We can never survey our own sentiments and motives, we can never form any judgment concerning them; unless we remove ourselves, as it were, from our own natural station, and endeavour to view them as at a certain distance from us. (128)

Imagining ourselves in the situation of a fair and impartial spectator enables us to form a balanced judgment. But that requires our having spectators. If a human creature grew up into some solitary place without any communication with fellow human beings, it would be impossible to think about his own character, sentiments, or conduct. "Bring him into society, and he is immediately provided with the mirror which he wanted before" (129).

Being able to sympathize and identify with the predicament of another person is a key precondition to solidarity. Only a self that mirrors the imagined viewpoints of others is capable of solidarity. Solidarity presupposes the double capacity to assess and appraise the self as well as to recognize the other, and it is conceivable that the individualization process has contributed to a change in exactly this respect. On the one hand, the self has become more uncertain and disoriented, rendering the appraisal and recognition of self as well as other more difficult. On the other hand, a characteristic of individualized citizens is their increased assertiveness. Since the 1960s, when the traditional structures of authority in family, education, work, and politics came under attack, the growing emphasis on personal autonomy, self-realization, and freedom of choice is assumed to have resulted in a much more assertive life-style (van den Brink 2001). The permissiveness of the 1960s, reflected in the socialization of children, would have created larger egos and a diminished capacity to imagine oneself in the position of another person and to feel responsible for the consequences of one's actions. According to Christopher Lasch (1979) this resulted in a growing narcissism and an increased vulnerability to infractions on immediate impulse satisfaction. This might explain why some people's tolerance for insignificant inconveniences in public life seems to have shrunk to zero: having to wait at a counter or a red light or having to show your ticket on the train may already be felt as a narcissistic offense and therefore an occasion for aggression.

Diversification and Uncertainty amid Strangers

Modern Western societies are increasingly multicultural and diverse in terms of ethnicity, sexual preferences, religious convictions, and cultural tastes. The set of shared, collective meanings is diminishing, and there is a growing diversity in social and cultural commitments. The individualized individual is faced with both a growing fluidity and fragmentation of his or her identity and an increased tendency to self-assertion and the suppression of other identities. The growing uncertainty of modern citizens makes the presence of the many "strangers" entering Western societies as refugees or immigrants potentially threatening. Strangers mean a lack of clarity: one does not know their habits and preferences, so suspicion is the most likely response to them. As long as they can be confined to their own quarters, it is easy to avoid them, but in this era of immigration, strangers are far too numerous to hold them at a "safe" distance.

Strangers have become a stable and irreversible part of our social world (Bauman 1997).

An almost prototypical form of solidarity is hospitality toward strangers. In the ancient virtue of hospitality, caring for the needs of the stranger was considered an inevitable obligation toward fellow human beings: there was a "general human obligation to hospitality" (Finley 1988: 101). The Bible ordains hospitality to strangers as a holy plight. In Homer's *Odyssey* the rule of hospitality was to welcome a guest in your home, offer him food and shelter, and only afterward ask questions about his person and mission. Hospitality was regarded as equivalent to the fundamental recognition and acceptance of "otherness," of plurality in the world. As such it can be seen as the basis of morality – "to be moral is to be hospitable to the stranger" (Ogletree 1985 [1946]: 1).

Contemporary hospitality has retained its obligatory character in many countries all over the world, particularly Third World countries, Asia, the Mediterranean countries, and Eastern Europe. When we lose our way in the Greek countryside and knock on the door of some small farmhouse, in nine out of ten cases you will be received in the most cordial way and be served the best food available in the house. The meaning of hospitality in these parts of the world is still related to reciprocity and mutual exchange: just as strangers may need you, you might need them at some other time, and therefore you should offer them hospitality (Pitt-Rivers 1968; Herzfeld 1987). However, in modern Western welfare states the original meaning of hospitality has changed. With the rise of welfare and individualism, strangers do not "need" one another any longer as they used to in ancient times. Whereas in the 1960s many Western welfare states started using foreigners as workers because they needed cheap labor, four decades later many of these workers have become "superfluous": we don't need them anymore. Another category of strangers, the refugees and the immigrants, need Western welfare states to secure shelter and a decent way of living, while a growing number of autochthonous people feel uneasy about the influx of strangers. The former reciprocity in the interaction between strangers and indigenous people has clearly been lost. Hospitality has become depersonalized and commercialized and has lost its original moral meaning of being obliged to take care of the needs of your fellow human beings, whoever they may be. An opposite development is that as a consequence of the increased global networks people have become less "strange" toward one another. The reciprocity of the classical hospitality has been substituted by new manifestations of worldwide connectedness.

Globalization and the New Society

Globalization, the growing interconnectedness of the world, includes many domains: the electronic transformation in communication and information (between universities, between nations and actors like political and military representatives, between companies doing business, etc.); the growth of a unifying, global culture, the development of a world economy, mass transport systems, a world system of tourism, and global social movements such as the human rights movement, the environmental movement, or the women's movement (B. Turner and Rojek 2001).

The new society has been variously labeled as a "network society" (Castells 1996) or a "risk society" (Beck 1986), to mention just a few influential contemporary approaches. In Castells's view the new information technologies by means of their pervasiveness and flexibility have created a universally integrated social world. He argues that transnational linkages of information, finance, and communication make the traditional conception of the nation-state obsolete. Instead, the network society emerges as the primary unit of sociological analysis. Networks differ from the old sociological units of the small group or the community in that the latter refer to exclusive and closed linkages, whereas the new networks are dynamic, inclusive, and open. The network society not only has a major effect on the development of capitalism and commerce but also invades the worlds of politics and culture. While it enables cooperation on a much wider scale and allows for instantaneous forms of reciprocity, many of the institutions constructed around the democratic state and around the contract between capital and labor have lost their meaning to individual people (B. Turner and Rojek 2001). Not only political institutions but also the sphere of work and production seem to be losing its force to bind citizens in solidarity.

The fact that information has become instantaneously available throughout the globe has enormous consequences. Bauman presents an interesting analysis of the impact of the changed role played by time and space for social cohesion. The former small-scale communities were "brought into being and kept alive by the gap between the nearly instantaneous communication *inside* the small-scale community . . . and the enormity of time and expense needed to pass information *between* localities" (Bauman 1998: 15). Nowadays, intracommunity communication has no advantage over intercommunal exchange, as both are instantaneous. Bauman describes how traditional societies were organized around the unmediated capacities of human bodies: "Conflict was chin-to-chin. Combat was hand-to-hand. Justice was an eye-for-an-eye, a tooth-for-a-tooth. Debate was heart-to-heart. Solidarity was shoulder-to-shoulder. Community was face-to-face. Friendship was arm-in-arm. And, change was step-by-step" (Bauman 1998: 17). All this has changed fundamentally with the advance of the means to stretch these interactions beyond the reach of the human eye and arm.

Although most globalization literature is concerned with money, labor, and markets, care can also become globalized. As care is a core aspect of solidarity, the phenomenon of what Arlie Hochschild calls "global care chains" is extremely interesting from our perspective. These chains are composed of "a series of personal links between people across the globe based on the paid or unpaid work of caring" (Hochschild 2000: 131). Women are usually making up these chains, although men may participate in them as well. The global chains usually go from poor to rich countries. They often connect three sets of caretakers: "[O]ne cares for the migrant's children back home, a second cares for the children of the woman who cares for the migrant's children, and a third, the migrating mother herself, cares for the children of professionals in the First World. Poorer women raise children for wealthier women while still poorer – or older or more rural – women raise their children" (136).

The globalization process creates new possibilities for solidarity but may also result in new forms of inequality, thereby putting new strains on solidarity. One paradoxical effect of globalization is that immediate reciprocity has diminished to the extent that justice, war, and democracy are not produced in face-to-face encounters any longer, while a new type of immediate, virtual reciprocity over the long distance has come into being.

Changes in Contemporary Solidarity

In the foregoing section a rather pessimistic tone has sometimes re-sounded: some of the authors cited seem to have a particularly keen eye for developments pointing to a decline. As Alan Wolfe (2000) has rightly pointed out, statements about a supposed social decline are problematic for various reasons. First, there is a problem of definition: what counts exactly as social decline? Second, there is a problem of measurement: in many cases it is very difficult to know whether certain acts are increasing because we do not have points of comparison with earlier periods. Third, generalization is problematic: on the basis of anecdotal information con-cerning particular behavior, generalizations are made about the state of society. Complaining about the moral quality of modern society might lead to excessive criticism of contemporary culture. Moreover, accounts of social decline always carry the risk of ignoring other developments that are of a qualitative rather than a quantitative nature. Solidarity may change in quality or nature, instead of being in decline. These considerations

tempted Wolfe even "to want the word *decline* banished from the literature. At least among social scientists notions of decline cause a reversal of
the proper way to examine a hypothesis" (2000: 130). Now we shift our
attention to more empirically based changes – in traditional solidarity,
local and global solidarity, and civil solidarity.

Traditional Solidarity

Since Durkheim's account of the change of mechanical into organic solidarity, the supposed decline of the binding force of family, neighborhood,
and church – sources of mechanical solidarity par excellence – has been
much discussed. It is certainly true that the extent to which mutual support was traditionally exchanged within families and neighborhoods has
diminished, although, as we have seen in Chapter 7, a firm basis of familial
solidarity has survived (Hareven 1995). In many European countries most
people still believe that the younger generation should contribute, financially or otherwise, to a decent standard of living for older or ill family
members, and informal care is still supplied on a large scale. As noted
in Chapter 6, traditional forms of solidarity – giving time to volunteer
work and providing care to people outside one's own household – are still
very much alive in the Netherlands. According to recent Dutch figures
no substantial decline of received informal care has occurred between
1979 and 1999, although this was expected as a consequence of women's
greater labor participation (SCP-Report 2002). The abstract and anonymous solidarity of giving to charity and to humanitarian goals is even
increasing in the Netherlands, as we have seen. The decline in religiosity
in Western society has undoubtedly diminished its binding force. In 1960
24% of the Dutch population said they were irreligious, but around the
turn of the century this has increased to 60% (SCP-Report 1998, 2002).
In the Western world new forms of spirituality and collective belief have
arisen, but these are often more individualistic and exert a lesser group
pressure compared with earlier forms of religion.

In the political commitment of Dutch citizens a double tendency seems to be at work. On the one hand, the membership in traditional forms of political organization such as political parties and labor unions has been declining steadily – but seems to be on the rise again since 2003 – and citizens are voting less often. This trend is also visible in other European countries (Zoll 2000). Whereas in 1965 9.7% of the Dutch still belonged to a political party, this share has been reduced to 2.4% in 1996 (SCP-Report 1998). At the beginning of the 1980s 39% of the population was a union member, but at the end of the 1990s this has declined to 30% (SCP-Report 2000). On the other hand, citizens indicate that their political interest has grown (van den Brink 2002). They increasingly agree with certain democratic liberties. Also political solidarity as expressed in participation in action groups or demonstrations has increased since 1977 (Dekker 2002).

Finally, collective expressions of solidarity without explicit political aims still occur regularly and may even be increasing; Durkheim (1964b [1895]) called these events "social currents." In 2002 the Netherlands has been alarmed by the politically inspired murder of the populist, right-wing politician Pim Fortuyn. The public expressed its emotions of sorrow and anger in large marches, while carrying candles and flowers. Other examples are the "White Marches" in Belgium, expressing compassion with the victims of child abuse and murder by Marc Dutroux, and the silent marches to mourn the victims of public violence. Contemporary citizens have not so much become less politically engaged but express their commitment differently (de Hart 1999; van den Brink 2002).

Local and Global Solidarity

Looking at local forms of solidarity, a multitude of new types present themselves. One fascinating example is the Local Exchange Trade System, or LETS. In LETS participants exchange services and goods without paying each other money. Instead one can "earn" and "pay" by means of exchange points. After the system was initiated in Canada in 1983, it has since begun to grow worldwide. In Europe LETS first developed in Britain during the 1990s. At the start of the new millennium in Britain about five hundred systems are operating. In the Netherlands by 2000 there are about one hundred systems, each system consisting of twenty-five to fifty participants. Dutch research has demonstrated that within one system yearly three hundred transactions take place, and 10,800 units are transacted (Hoeben 2000). Reciprocity, or delayed reciprocity, is an essential element in LETS: I do something for you and, although you may not do something in return immediately, at a future moment somebody will do something for me. The idea of reinforcing community by exchanging goods and services is crucial to LETS: exchange is promoting social connectedness and stimulates the community feeling that is believed to be on the decline in modern society. Reciprocity, solidarity, and connectedness are key concepts in LETS.

Several other forms of local and informal solidarity have arisen in Western society. To say that these forms are completely new would not be correct, as they have always existed. However, their number seems to have increased and their focus may be new. We can think of the well-known self-help groups, having their origins in the United States, and spreading all over Europe since the 1970s. Since the 1980s and 1990s new forms of reciprocal aid have been initiated in the Netherlands and in many other countries (Zoll 2000), of which the buddy system – homosexuals helping fellow homosexuals having AIDS – is the best known. Former psychiatric patients, delinquents, handicapped, or chronically ill people help others who share their fate. An interesting aspect of the way aspirant buddies are trained is the explicit recognition of the element of self-interest involved in providing support and help to a partner in misfortune (Komter 2000). The underlying idea of these projects is that solidarity is not effective anymore when an exclusive appeal is made to the altruism and selflessness of volunteers; only when it is clear that they have something to gain from providing help themselves will they make their contribution to solidarity.

Thus the reciprocity aspect of solidarity – always a part of it but remaining implicit for long – is made explicit and visible.

Another relatively new form of solidarity, also based on reciprocity, is located in the daily interaction among citizens in their own neighborhoods. In some of the big cities in the Netherlands the local authorities have initiated projects aimed at improving the quality of life within particular urban, often multiculturally populated areas, characterized by high levels of unemployment, poverty, poor housing conditions, criminality, and mutual distrust. By creating the material and institutional conditions enabling citizens to invest in the quality of their own immediate surroundings, the local authorities hope to promote mutual reciprocity and solidarity. Enabling people to make their own choices and to realize their autonomy is viewed as a promising strategy to enhance mutual trust and foster community feelings. For instance, in Rotterdam, a project called City etiquette aims at enhancing public courtesy and mutual respect, and in the city of Gouda the authorities have proclaimed the "ten city rules" with a similar purpose.

Also on a global level solidarity takes on a new shape. The era of globalization and the new means of communication open up new possibilities for developing shared interests, forms of community, and solidarity in transnational social movements (Smith, Chatfield, and Pagnucco 1997; Cohen and Rai 2000). Examples are international nongovernmental organizations, the Worldwide Fund for Nature, and the Friends of the Earth. World summits are organized on the environment, social development, and population issues. On the Internet worldwide chat and information exchange create new alliances and partnerships. New interest groups manifest their political views, or other convictions and programs, and initiate new appeals to solidarity. Due to the diversity and rapid development of these new forms of global solidarity, it is impossible to formulate a general assessment of their impact. But it is beyond doubt that the new global solidarity has created unprecedented possibilities for developing new identifications and social ties.

Civil Solidarity

For a long period of time the concepts of civility and civilization re-
ferred to "the self-image of the European upper class in relation to others
whom its members considered simpler or more primitive" (Elias 1978:
39). Civilization was thought of as the privilege of the elite, and civilized
behavior was viewed as the distinctive characteristic of the upper classes.
In the nineteenth and the first decades of the twentieth century those
at the bottom of society, the poor and the unemployed, were the object
of initiatives aimed at their "civilization." Against this background it is
understandable that in the 1960s talking about civility was seen as tantamount to being a snob or a reactionary. With the growth of democratic
culture and the rise of a more informal style of behavior during the past
decades, the concepts of civilization and civility lost their elitist stigma.
Civility came to be understood as the "the civil treatment of others and
respect for their sensibilities" (Misztal 2001: 72). Nowadays an increasing
concern with civility can be observed. Civil society, modern citizenship,
and the respect toward fellow citizens are thought to be diminishing.
In the United States the decline of civility is bemoaned by scholars like
Bennett (1993), Carter (1998), Lane (2000), and Putnam (2000).

Coming back to Alan Wolfe's warnings about talk of decline and problems of definition, it seems worthwhile to study the notion of civility in
some more detail. One of the meanings of civility – manners, politeness –
can be traced back to the seminal work on the civilization process in
Western societies by Norbert Elias (1978). He showed that this meaning
of civility has its origins in medieval courtesy, the behavior required at
the court. In the course of the civilization process the former external
social constraints were converted into self-control and self-regulation of
spontaneous impulses. Self-control emerges here as an important aspect
of civility, in addition to manners. However, civility has deeper meanings
than the rather superficial one of courtesy and manners. Edward Shils
(1991), for instance, considers civility an essential virtue that implies our

recognition of the humanity of self and others and a willingness – based on an awareness of mutual dependency – to develop communality with others. Respect and care for fellow citizens are important elements in this conception (see also Dekker 2000). Conceived this way the concept of civility is closely related to solidarity. Indeed, various scholars conceive of civility as a form of solidarity, taking shape in concrete local settings in which citizens interact with one another (Cahoone 2000a; Misztal 2001). According to Virginia Straus (2000) civility and civil society are founded on a minimal dignity for all citizens: "Civility in civil society means regarding others as members of the same inclusive collectivity and respecting them as such. Even one's enemies must be included in this same moral universe. In addition, civility describes the conduct of a person who has a concern for the good of the whole society" (Straus 2000: 230).

Because of the similarity between the concepts of civility and solidarity, in what follows I use the concept of "civil solidarity," which comprises the following four characteristics: self-restraint, or the control of spontaneous impulses and of the desire for immediate gratification; good manners, or not being rude; being aware of other people as fellow human beings and treating them accordingly; and willingness to subordinate private concerns to public interests.

If we look at solidarity thus conceived, a variety of behaviors indeed seems to indicate a decline of civil solidarity in either one of these meanings, or a combination of them. The increase in (criminal and other) violence is perhaps the best illustration. As in most other European countries, in the Netherlands statistical data unequivocally point to an increase in criminal violence during the past decades (SCP-Report 2000). Two decades after 1975 the number of violent crimes has increased by a factor of three; in the same period also physical ill-treatment shows a rise. In particular, violence by youthful perpetrators has increased. Vandalism has quadrupled between 1975 and 1995 (van den Brink 2001). The amount of destruction has increased since 1990, both in the perception of citizens themselves and in police records. There is more aggression in schools, in traffic, in the office of the general practitioner, in hospitals, and in social service departments. At Columbine High School in the United States and also in Erfurt in Germany, pupils cold-bloodedly shot their teachers and fellow pupils to death out of anger and frustration toward the school. To explain this type of violence, we might again refer to the overwhelming centrality of the need for self-recognition in modern citizens. As a consequence the vulnerability to narcissistic offenses, and thus the tendency to respond with aggression, have risen considerably. Unfortunately no longitudinal data are available to substantiate the assumptions about the grown ego and the assertive self. Dutch data from a research done in 1997 do, however, show that citizens think personal qualities such as independence and standing up for yourself are more important than being able to take the imaginary position of other people and to cooperate with them (SCP-Report 2002: 60). If we add to this the numerous special issues of newspapers and weekly magazines about public impertinence that have appeared in the Netherlands over the past years, we can conclude that the need for recognition and assertion of the self has become a predominant motivation among many contemporary citizens, leaving no room for the recognition of others.

Modern traffic, with its anonymity and high potential for developing aggressive feelings, is another domain where the diminishing civil solidarity can be observed. Raising the middle finger as an expression of one's anger and contempt for other people, tailgating and honking incessantly, ignoring the red light oneself and being angry at others who start driving when the light is green, obstructing ticket control in public transport by becoming violent – all these examples show a decline in civil solidarity. An extremely disconcerting development is the increase in the number of people who drive on after having caused an accident. Figures from the Dutch Ministry of Internal Affairs show that between 1990 and 1999 the number of police warrants related to driving on after an accident has doubled. We can only guess at the motives of the perpetrators: lack of consideration for the victim and alcohol abuse are candidates, in addition to the relatively low chance of being caught anyhow.

A relatively new phenomenon connected to the spread of the cell phone is the habit of conducting overly loud private conversations in public, for example, in trains or other public spaces, thereby preventing other people from continuing their silent reading, thinking, or sleeping. Although not as aggressive as the earlier mentioned examples, this practice nevertheless shows a lack of civil solidarity as we have defined it earlier: the possible needs and wishes of fellow citizens are ignored.

Yet another sign of declining civil solidarity is the disrespect shown in dealing with public space: leaving rubbish in public parks and on the streets instead of using the dustbin, or urinating in public instead of using the public rest room. In many big cities, and not exclusively in the Netherlands, the signs of pollution and neglect of the public space are clearly visible.

It must be emphasized at this point that these developments should be seen in the historical context of the second half of the twentieth century. The supposed decline of civil solidarity only pertains to the period since the 1950s. We should have no illusions whatsoever about civil solidarity in former ages when robber bands were terrorizing the countryside and the big cities were far from safe and clean.

Transformed Solidarity

Significant changes have occurred in contemporary solidarity. At the beginning of the twenty-first century the traditional mechanical solidarity of family, neighborhood, and church has diminished, but not completely disappeared. The significance of religion has diminished but new forms of spirituality have come into being. Family solidarity still has firm roots, as is shown in substantial intergenerational solidarity. The solidarity of informal care and volunteer work remains at the same level in the Netherlands, as in most other European countries. The abstract solidarity of donating to charity and membership of humanitarian organizations is yearly increasing. The political engagement of Dutch citizens shows a double tendency: less commitment to traditional political organizations and a growing involvement outside these organizations. Also collective solidarity manifestations without political goals seem to be increasing. Many new forms of solidarity have made their appearance. Participants to the Local Exchange Trade Systems, now rapidly spreading over Europe, are establishing social connectedness and community feelings by mutually exchanging help and services. Furthermore, many self-help groups and groups offering reciprocal aid have arisen as people sharing a common fate provide support for each other. In big cities local authorities encourage citizens to contribute to the livability of their own neighborhoods. Also global solidarity is increasing: new social movements and new interest groups exchange services and create social bonds through the Internet. There are indications of a decline in civil solidarity, at least since the 1950s.

On the basis of the findings presented in this chapter it has become clear that it is impossible to speak in any general terms about a decline or an increase in contemporary solidarity. Some forms have diminished, others have remained at the same level, and yet others have increased. Moreover, a multitude of new forms of solidarity has come into existence. It is interesting to note that Michael Schudson has reached a similar conclusion in his book *The Good Citizen* (2000). He shows that in the United States the decline in citizenship as supposed by Putnam and others is only partly true. On certain dimensions of citizenship there is an increase instead of a decline. We can conclude that solidarity has diversified, with regard not only to the types that can be distinguished but also to patterns of increase or decrease. The number of new solidarity initiatives is hopeful and does not warrant a gloomy picture about contemporary solidarity. One specific domain of solidarity, however, that gives rise to some concern is civil solidarity, which can determine the quality of the public domain and of social life to a large extent.

∽

NINE

Solidarity and the Gift

Not satisfied with a society fashioned by uncoordinated individual efforts, one of humanity's greatest accomplishments is
to translate egocentric community concerns into collective values. The desire for a modus vivendi fair to everyone may be
regarded as an evolutionary outgrowth of the need to get along
and cooperate, adding an ever-greater insight into the actions
that contribute to or interfere with this objective.

(Frans de Waal 1996: 207)

The classical sociological question about the bases of social order is of
great current interest. In our times there is a concern about the fate
of solidarity and social ties similar to that at the end of the nineteenth
century. In both eras significant social transformations were presumably
affecting the "cement of society." In the preceding chapters we returned
to the works of the classical anthropologists and sociologists, as well as to
more modern theories. Once again the classics proved invaluable to our
understanding of the complexity of the current "problem of order."

It is remarkable that so few attempts have been made to bridge anthropological and sociological theories on social ties and solidarity. In
the same period that Durkheim described the transformation from mechanical to organic solidarity, anthropologists conducted detailed field
studies about the origin of human societies in diverging cultures: from
North American Indian tribes to the Maori tribes in New Zealand and the

inhabitants of the Trobriand Islands. Whereas the sociologists emphasized the shared values and norms and the new forms of mutual dependency that the modernizing society brought about, the anthropologists conceived of solidarity as the consequence of patterns of reciprocity between individuals, arising from the exchange of gifts and services.

In this chapter we investigate what the conditions are under which contemporary solidarity comes into being and has positive or negative consequences. In addition, an attempt is made to understand and explain the essence of the transformation solidarity has gone through. But first, we look back upon the preceding chapters, in order to see where their main conclusions have brought us.

The Gift: Meanings and Motives

In Part I of this book we studied the basic meanings on which gift exchange is founded. In Chapter 1 things were analyzed as developing meaning in the context of social interaction and mutual communication between people. Things evoke various emotions in people. Human beings expose things to an "exchange of sacrifices" by exchanging them with others. The value and meaning of things is derived from their "sacrifice" in exchange rituals. Four broad categories of meaning, based on Alan Page Fiske's models of social relationships, are affectivity, with solidarity and friendship as keywords; asymmetry and power inequality, in which one's status or power in relationships with other people is emphasized; equality between those involved in a relationship; and instrumentality, with self-interest, competition, and struggle as central notions. By focusing our analysis on gifts as one important category of things, we confirmed the four broad-meaning categories by some empirical data on gift exchange. An important element in gift giving is the concept of sacrifice; in a gift not only is an object sacrificed but also the identity of the giver or recipient may be sacrificed in the exchange.

Chapter 2 addressed the social and psychological patterns of giving and receiving. The principle of reciprocity proved to be effective in the "archaic" societies studied by anthropologists and also in gift exchange in a Western society (in this case the Netherlands). The mutual recognition of the identity of giver and recipient is the precondition for gift exchange. Reciprocal recognition of other human beings, of their general human worth as well as of their individual person and identity, seems also to be the moral basis for solidarity, even though this is not stated explicitly in theories on solidarity. Fiske's four relational models can again be recognized in some empirical data about motives to give. Although not completely covering all the motives reported, affectivity, equality, power, and instrumentality again prove to be basic motivational dimensions of gift giving. Gifts can be both positive and negative; they can create as well as disturb or undermine social ties.

In Chapter 3 we saw that the cycle of gift and countergift is sustained by means of gratitude. Gratitude has a spiritual, magical, or religious layer expressed in the mainly non-Western idea that people are part of a natural cycle and should give back to nature what riches they have taken from it. In a second layer, gratitude is conceived as a moral virtue and an important aspect of character. The third and fourth layers consist of the social and cultural meanings of gratitude: gratitude as the moral basis of both reciprocity and social bonds, and of community and a shared culture. In theories on social ties and solidarity the concept of gratitude is notoriously absent, even though gratitude is the core of the reciprocal moral obligation involved in many instances of solidarity. Family solidarity, for instance, is often inspired by a generalized sense of gratitude (also called delayed reciprocity): my parents have raised me and given me so much; now it is my turn to care for them. And, at least as common, the lack of gratitude due to the parents' failure to contribute to one's own well-being can turn into anger and resentment, and act as a forceful motive to refrain from solidarity.

Chapter 4 focused on the gendered meaning of gift giving. Because women are the more generous gift givers, the analysis considered the still existing power inequality between men and women that results from the difference in their disposable material and nonmaterial resources. Women and men benefit alternatively from women's greater generosity. On the one hand, men may derive certain benefits from being less involved in gift giving than women: they are less constrained by the obligations connected to the "gift work" while at the same time receiving numerous gifts themselves. For women, the risk of gift giving (remember that not only material gifts but also nonmaterial ones were included in the analysis) may be to lose their own autonomy and identity by being overly self-sacrificing. On the other hand, women's greater share in gift giving may yield them some substantial advantages. Through their gift giving women are the prime intermediaries in creating and affirming social ties, which, presumably, result in social capital. Women are more accustomed than men to express their concern for other people in concrete acts of benevolence, and this can act as a boomerang so that they will proportionally receive concern and benevolence in return. Women play a significant role in the production and maintenance of the social texture of our society. In some of its manifestations, then, solidarity is clearly gendered.

Solidarity and Selectivity

In Part II of this book the focus shifted from the various meanings associated with gift giving to the classical anthropological and sociological theories on solidarity and to some concrete cases of solidarity. In particular, Part II drew attention to some negative aspects of solidarity.

In Chapter 5 we observed that compared with the overwhelming attention the aspect of reciprocity has received from the gift theorists, in sociological theory it is clearly undervalued. A second, returning theme concerns motives for solidarity. The anthropological theories proved to offer a broader range of possible motives than the work of the classical sociologists: from the "pure" gift given to close relatives, through equivalent reciprocity, to forms of exchange based on self-interest. Anthropologists point to another important motive that may be involved in creating and maintaining social order: power. Gifts can serve as instruments of power, status, and honor and be used to fortify one's own position and to protect oneself against the risks implied in ties with rivals. The theory of the gift revealed the same four motives to engage in social relationships as had already been discussed in Chapter 1. A final theme relevant to our subject matter is ritual. The symbolism involved in ritual, the awareness and recognition of the identity of the other, and the shared norms and common emotional mood required by the ritual all contribute to reinforcing social bonds. Just as the participants of the Kula ritual who did not comply with the conventions of the gift ceremonials were sanctioned by social disapproval and excommunication, also in our own society not abiding by the symbolic codes of rituals is to disturb the bond of alliance and community.

Chapter 6 brought a new element into the picture, that of "negative solidarity," solidarity acting as a principle of selection or exclusion. Although there is no reason for serious concern about contemporary solidarity as expressed in charity, volunteer work, or informal care, there are some inherent failures of solidarity. Empirical data about gift giving show that those who give much also receive much, whereas poor givers are poor recipients as well. A Matthew effect is at work, benefiting the most generous givers and disadvantaging those who are already in poor social and material conditions. Reciprocity ties people together but may simultaneously act as a principle of exclusion. Empirical data on informal care suggests that primarily family and close relatives profit from this care. Solidarity is selective in that relatives and family are preferred above those who are farther away in social distance. Philanthropic particularism, the inherent tendency of voluntary initiatives to favor those with whom one identifies most, again echoes the negative side of solidarity.

In Chapter 7 family solidarity was investigated in more detail. Family solidarity has traditionally been considered the prototype of Durkheim's mechanical solidarity, the small homogeneous community firmly rooted in shared values and characterized by a natural propensity to display solidarity toward its members. In our individualized society this solidarity is assumed to be in decline, or at least to have become less self-evident. Empirical data presented in this chapter, however, suggest that the broadly felt concern about the vitality of family bonds and intergenerational solidarity is not warranted. People are still willing to contribute, financially or otherwise, to the care needed by the elderly. In particular, women are still providing a substantial amount of informal care, especially to older generations. A solid base for family solidarity has remained but there are also signs that the motivation for family solidarity is predominantly based on "prescribed altruism," an inner obligation to care, rather than on feelings of affection and identification. Moreover, family ties are often ambivalent and based on contradictory feelings.

Contemporary Solidarity

Whereas the first seven chapters highlighted various classical and more modern theories on gift giving as well as solidarity, in Chapter 8 the focus was on changes in contemporary solidarity. Various cultural critics have propounded rather gloomy views about the consequences of the individualization process for contemporary citizenship. Individuals are thought to be less committed to politics as an institution and to the attainments of the welfare state; they are assumed to be less able to engage in longer-term projects and relationships, and their life course has become more fragmented. As a consequence of individualization and the increased diversity of social and cultural identities and involvements people's uncertainty about their own identity and place in the world has grown. This uncertainty may increase still more, due to the arrival of "strangers" in many Western societies. In addition, the 1960s has created a self that is more assertive than ever before and that tends to reinforce itself above other selves. Against these possibly negative developments, new opportunities to form social ties and develop solidarity have been created by the globalization process. In the second part of this chapter the attention shifted to more empirically based changes in solidarity in Western societies. The picture proved varied: some forms of traditional solidarity have diminished but others are on the rise, and also new forms of solidarity can be observed. It is therefore impossible to speak in general terms about a decrease or increase of solidarity. The many new initiatives and the solid base of many traditional forms of solidarity do not give rise to gloominess about contemporary solidarity, as we concluded in Chapter 8. The observed decline in civil solidarity, though, does warrant some concern.

At this point, we return to the central question of this book: how can the combined insights derived from the theories on the gift and on solidarity contribute to our understanding of both the positive and the negative manifestations of contemporary solidarity? From the anthropological and sociological literature four relevant dimensions emerge: recognition of otherness, social distance, motives for solidarity, and reciprocity.

Solidarity and the Gift

Recognition of the Other

The anthropological theory of the gift can be considered a theory of human solidarity, as we have seen. The principle of reciprocity underlying gift exchange proved to be the fundament of human society. It contains the moral basis for the development of social ties and solidarity because its implicit assumption is the recognition of the other person as a potential ally. The social and cultural system on which archaic societies were based rested on the mutual acceptance of the other as a partner in gift exchange. Recognition of the other as a human being proves to be an essential precondition for the coming into being of patterns of exchange. Without recognition of the person and his or her identity no reciprocal exchange is possible.

The significance of recognition of the other returns in the accounts of both contemporary and classical thinkers. For instance, Honneth (1992) conceives of reciprocity as an issue of recognition. In order to be able to feel self-respect, people need the respect and regard of others. We recognize Adam Smith's and George Herbert Mead's views on the mirroring of the imaginary viewpoint of the other in our own minds. Honneth distinguishes between three forms of intersubjective recognition – through love, life, and law – resulting in three layers of self-regard. In love people are experiencing a fundamental sense of being valued as an individual. In social life humans are valued and respected because of personal characteristics that are socially valued. In law, finally, people are valued regardless of their personal characteristics and regardless of the social value of these characteristics. Similarly Habermas (1989) regards identity as the result of processes of mutual recognition, and reciprocal recognition as a basic assumption underlying solidarity. According to him the basic principles of modern solidarity are not fundamentally different from the mutual expectations of reciprocity existing in premodern societies.

Also in Hannah Arendt's view (1978) adoption of the plurality of other people's viewpoints in our own minds is the only way to transcend our own, interest-driven self and the limitations of our own judgment. In addition, Arendt provides us with some poignant premonitions concerning the emotions on which solidarity is sometimes built. Compassion and pity with the societal underclasses are often important motives within revolutionary movements. In *On Revolution* (1963) she presents a fascinating analysis of the role of solidarity and pity during the French Revolution. The revolutionaries, with Robespierre in their vanguard, were driven by pity for the mass of the poor and exploited people; they idealized the poor and praised their suffering as a source of virtue. The revolutionaries' pity became a pretext for the exercise of brute power, resulting in the ruthless annihilation of the opponents of the revolution. The revolutionary solidarity was based on a lack of recognition of others as human beings and of the plurality of their viewpoints.

Recognition of the humanity of self and other is tantamount to recognition of the interdependency of self and other. For the recognition of humanity implies that other people's needs and their mutual dependency for the fulfillment of these needs are recognized. In Chapter 8 we argued that the psychological development of the assertive self may be at odds with the capacity to recognize the other and the awareness of mutual dependency. The precarious position of civil solidarity can largely be explained by the fact that its fundamental precondition – recognition of otherness – seems to be subject to erosion.

Social Distance

Recognition of other people's human worth is directly related to the next dimension: social distance. From the work of the classical anthropologists it appeared that the nature of the gift was related to the nature of the social relationship: the closer the distance – family, relatives – the more disinterested the gift and the less specific the expectations of return gifts: I give to you, but I do not care so much about when or even if I receive something back. In relations with unknown people gifts given out of motives of personal gain or self-interest are more likely. In between lies a more or less equal or equivalent exchange of gifts: everybody gives and receives, and nobody gains or loses by it. Similarly, Georg Simmel (1950 [1908]) reflected on the way solidarity was related to social distance. In his view solidarity would be transformed as a consequence of individualization. As the traditional forms of community would lose their binding force, people would increasingly be able to regard their fellow human beings as representatives of the human species in general rather than a particular group or culture. According to Simmel the process of individualization would lead to more extended identifications; the new solidarity would cover larger collectivities and become more abstract in nature (van Oorschot et al. 2001).

Solidarity has indeed become more global and abstract, as we have seen. Worldwide networks and interest groups, new global solidarity movements, and the growing willingness to give to charity and support humanitarian goals seem to confirm Simmel's ideas about the rise of abstract solidarity. However, such abstract solidarity is "easier" than concrete solidarity in the form of care and support to fellow human beings, because one is less directly confronted with the effects of poverty, illness, or hunger. Filling in a bank check for some charity requires less personal identification and less effort than caring for an ill relative. No real disaster is imminent when a member of a worldwide network does not live up to his or her commitments. The anonymity of global solidarity is at the same time its strength and its weakness. The lack of direct personal responsibility and the low level of personal and emotional commitment facilitate the mobilization of large numbers of people and the rapid growth of such networks, but they reduce solidarity to the exchange of information, consciousness raising, or a simple donation. Such a "thin" solidarity, as B. Turner and Rojek call it (2001), can never emulate the "thick" solidarity based on personal responsibility and commitment toward concrete human beings.

However, the thick solidarity occurring between kin and near relatives has a darker side as well, which becomes apparent in the selectivity of solidarity, as we have seen. In his book *Good Natured* (1996) Frans de Waal presents convincing proof for this selectivity among both humans and animal species. Human sympathy is restricted and is given most readily to one's own family and clan, and only reluctantly to the outside world, if at all. "Human history furnishes ample evidence that moral principles are oriented to one's own group, and only reluctantly (and never even-handedly) applied to the outside world. Standing on the medieval walls of a European city, we can readily imagine how tightly life within the walls was regulated and organised, whereas outsiders were only important enough to be doused with boiling oil" (1996: 30). This can to a large extent be explained by the well-known evolution principles, which predominantly serve the protection and survival of one's own family and close relatives. "Kindness towards one's kin is viewed as a genetic investment, a way of spreading genes similar to one's own. Assisting kin thus comes close to helping oneself" (de Waal 2001: 317).

Contemporary solidarity is an interesting mixture of thick and thin, both showing strengths and weaknesses.

Motives for Solidarity

In classical sociological theory solidarity motives were thought to be either inspired by affectivity and shared norms and values, or by instrumental considerations like self-interest and rational choice. An example of the first is the emotional commitment people feel toward their close relatives; solidarity based on self-interest becomes visible, for instance, in the collective arrangements of the welfare state: contributing collectively is to the advantage of every individual citizen. A striking difference between anthropological and sociological theory is the anthropologists' attention paid to the principle of give-and-take, whereby each individual gives about equally. The best illustration of the enormous significance of this equality motive is still found in the anthropological literature on gift exchange. Malinowski's account of the Kula shows that the bulk of the transactions between the inhabitants of the Trobriand Islands are of the equality type. As noted in Chapter 2, it appears that also in Western society the most common pattern is that the gift is followed by a more or less equal countergift. The underlying motivation is in Mauss's terms *do ut des*, I give so that you give in return. This is also the basis of the many forms of mutual help and types of local solidarity discussed in Chapter 8. Perhaps the "normalcy" of this type of solidarity is the reason why it has received such scarce attention in the sociological literature.

Another possible motivation for solidarity particularly emphasized by anthropologists is power. Both Mauss and Lévi-Strauss showed how the power motive could be involved in gift exchange: gifts can serve to reinforce the personal prestige and status of the giver, but also to humiliate or dominate the other party by putting him in a position of debt and dependence. Later these insights were elaborated upon by the sociologist Gouldner, but the anthropologists had clearly preceded him. It is obvious that power can be a forceful motive sustaining mutual solidarity, but there are various shades. A very strong internal group loyalty does not necessarily lead to the exercise of power and oppression. Thinking in terms of "us" and "them" can be observed in rival football clubs but also in groups with different religious convictions or cultural backgrounds. The relationship between the autochthonous population and the newcomers in Western societies illustrates the possible consequences. The more one exclusively identifies with one's own group and refrains from interaction with outsiders, the more negative effects on the outside world the intragroup solidarity will have, and the less the willingness to engage in intergroup cooperation and trust.

Groups tied by strong ethnic or nationalist identifications, as it were, need inimical other groups for their own survival. Their self-identification derives its legitimacy from the identification of other groups as the enemy. In extreme cases hate can breed the lust for power. The aim of the group becomes self-preservation through the oppression of outsiders by means of violence and destruction. The former Yugoslavia is one of the many examples showing how nationalist or ethnic pride and strong mutual solidarity can turn into ethnic cleansing and violent oppression. In his book *Blood and Belonging* (1993) Michael Ignatieff explores the numerous forms of new tribalism and nationalism in our globalized world. The use of violence is legitimized by the perceived threat to self-determination or the love for one's own blood and soil. The latter legitimization is perhaps the most convincing as it appeals to the supposedly better parts of human nature. In Ignatieff's words: "But if nationalism legitimizes an appeal to blood loyalty, and in turn blood sacrifice, it can only do so persuasively if it seems to appeal to people's better natures, and not just to their worst instincts. Since killing is not a business to be taken lightly, it must be done for a reason which makes its perpetrator think well of himself. If violence is to be legitimated, it must be in the name of all that is best in a people, and what is better than their love of home?" (1993: 6). Solidarity springing from feelings of "blood and belonging" is the most perverted of all solidarities. Self-interest is not a sufficient motive to explain this type of solidarity. The need to protect one's own group ideals and identity by oppressing others through exercising power and using violence is predominant here. This type of solidarity is based on the complete denial of the humanness of the other party.

Different from what modern sociology suggests, four broad categories of motives seem to underlie solidarity: affection, equality, power, and instrumentality or self-interest. Solidarity theory, then, would gain by adding equality and power to the more common motives of affectivity and instrumentality.

Reciprocity: Gift and Sacrifice

The fourth dimension, reciprocity, can take two shapes: gift and sacrifice. This dimension varies mainly in the degree of anonymity and abstractness of what is coming in return. Reciprocity and mutual sharing have a long history in social theory. In Auguste Comte's view, sociology was the scientific study of friendship and companionship (*socius*), the latter term pointing to the importance of sharing basic resources such as bread (*panis*) in order to be able to form and maintain social ties. Companionship is best exemplified by the communal sharing of a meal and the exchange of food, as is also reflected in the etymological roots of the word (B. Turner and Rojek 2001). The ritual of hospitality, the sharing of bread and other food, is a prototypical example of the morality of reciprocity. The essence is that receiving prompts giving.

Lévi-Strauss (1961 [1949]) gives an illuminating example in his account of a ceremonial aspect of the meal. In some lower-price restaurants in the south of France each guest finds a small bottle of wine in front of his plate. The bottle is the same as that of this person's neighbor at the table and holds just one glass. The contents of the bottle are not poured in the glass of the owner but in that of his neighbor, and the latter makes the gesture of reciprocity by doing exactly the same. In the end each guest has not received more than if he had consumed his own wine. Instead of silently sitting next to each other as strangers, social bond is created by the simple act of reciprocal wine pouring. It is impossible to refuse that gesture without appearing insulting. As a result not only the wine is returned but conversation is offered in return as well. This apparently futile scene represents a very basic situation: that in which individuals enter into contact with strangers and are facing the problem of either being friendly and establishing a bond or refusing to accept the stranger as a potential ally altogether. Lévi-Strauss spends several pages on this example because he feels that it offers "material for inexhaustible sociological reflection." He apparently shares Comte's view that studying reciprocity and the formation of social bonds should remain a concern for sociology.

Of course, not every exchange contains the moral element that leads to the formation of social ties. Purely economic exchange is not offering the moral context needed for the coming into existence of social bonds. As Frans de Waal rightly observes: "Reciprocity can exist without morality; there can be no morality without reciprocity" (1996: 136). Like Lévi-Strauss, de Waal thinks that the link between morality and reciprocity is particularly evident in hospitality and food sharing. "A link between morality and reciprocity is nowhere as evident as in the distribution of resources, such as the sharing of food. To invite others for dinner . . . and to have the invitation returned on a later date is a universally understood human ritual of hospitality and friendship" (de Waal 1996: 136). Apparently, a situation of reciprocity and sharing offers the best guarantee for a peaceful being together. Hospitality, or the sharing of a meal, seems to be the epitome of human community.

Why is the informal social contract created by reciprocity so effective in creating the cement of society? The answer lies in the sublime reconciliation of individual and social interests resulting from it. Its evolutionary effectivity has been amply documented in the work of biologists like Trivers (1971), in de Waal's animal studies, and in Malinowski's and Lévi-Strauss's anthropological field studies. Reciprocity represents the elegant combination of self-interested concerns with the requirements of social life. As Marcel Mauss said, "Material and moral life, and exchange, function . . . in a form that is both disinterested and obligatory" (1990 [1923]: 33).

Why is the concept of reciprocity more promising as a cornerstone of solidarity theory than is the basic assumption of rational choice theory that humans are rational egoists (Hechter 1987; Coleman and Fararo 1992)? It is because this assumption leaves no room for the aspect of moral obligation. Although people certainly try to realize their own best interests in many instances, there is more to human life than mere self-interest. Leaving aside the various other criticisms that can be launched against some of the core aspects of rational choice theory (Sen 1979; Coleman and Fararo 1992), the fact that people feel morally committed to their fellow human beings because they have given them something of value is ignored in contemporary rational choice–inspired theories of solidarity.

The notion of sacrifice is yet another significant aspect of solidarity that is generally overlooked in sociological theories; in the anthropological gift theory, however, it is a recurring theme (Hubert and Mauss 1974; Girard 1993 [1977]; Berking 1999). In the words of the German sociologist and anthropologist Berking, "It is not only that, in the most varied cultures, gifts are again and again understood as sacrifices and vice versa. It is also that gift and sacrifice denote two, admittedly distinguishable, intensities in the continuum of an anthropology of giving" (1999: 51). Throughout the centuries people in the most different cultures have sacrificed to gods or ancestors. Not only animals but occasionally also human beings were involved in ritual slaughter. An example showing the continuity between gift and sacrifice is the willingness of human beings to sacrifice their own lives in order to save another human being – rescuing a child from a burning house or preventing a person from drowning. Those who offered shelter to Jews during the Second World War to save them from Nazi prosecution put themselves at a serious, sometimes life-threatening risk. All these examples show a personal sacrifice occurring in the context of a concrete relationship with one or more other human beings (not necessarily being acquainted with one another).

The sacrifice of human lives does not only happen at the level of inter-personal relationships but also at that of groups, communities, clans, and nations. In the former case the sacrifice is concrete and personal, whereas in the case of large-scale group solidarity it is abstract and anonymous. This type of sacrifice can vary from the sacrifice of individual autonomy and freedom of thinking in the name of a certain group ideal, but group solidarity can also lead to the sacrifice of anonymous others' lives, because they have different convictions or a different group identity. An extremely high loyalty toward one's own group combined with extreme animosity and hate toward outsiders can lead one to sacrifice one's own life and that of as many enemies as possible, in order to attain personal martyrdom and heroism. The Muslim extremists who crashed planes into the twin towers of the World Trade Center on 11 September 2001 and the Palestinians who attack Israel by killing themselves provide examples of what Durkheim (1951 [1897]) called altruistic suicide: the sacrifice of one's own life for a "good cause."

Although the ideology of sacrifice does occur both at the interpersonal and the group level, the large-scale sacrifice of human lives is more char-acteristic for group solidarity than for relationships between individuals. Ideals of sacrifice have a prominent place in the consciousness of those who are unified in political or ethnic group solidarity. The stronger the value the group represents to its members, the more important it is to preserve internal cohesion. In communist groups and organizations it was a sign of political virtue to sacrifice one's personal interests and personal life to the political cause (Withuis 1990). Groups sharing a strong ideology are characteristically denying the validity of deviating beliefs and perspectives. The idea of sacrifice is a built-in feature of their belonging to the group and a fundament of the group as such.

This type of solidarity is more often found at the other pole of the reciprocity continuum. At this pole the type of reciprocity is different from the one belonging to the gift. Where more or less equivalent, concrete, and personal reciprocity is predominant with the gift, the reciprocity of sacrifice is of a nonequivalent, abstract, and impersonal nature: the sacrifice of individuality, autonomy, or human lives is reciprocated with abstractions like mutual loyalty and ideological purity, collective interest, or martyrdom. Whereas the gift is recompensed with a countergift, sacrifice yields heroism and a sense of moral superiority in return.

Toward a Theoretical Model of Solidarity

In the preceding sections I have argued that four dimensions are quintessential when trying to understand the various forms of solidarity. These dimensions provide the organizing principle in Figure 9.1, which comprises the different positive and negative manifestations of solidarity. Before explaining the details of the theoretical model, I want, first, to make a remark on ritual. In Chapter 5 the significance of ritual for solidarity was demonstrated. We saw how the rituals of the religious sacrifice and the shared meal served to create bonds between humans and gods and among humans. In contemporary society rituals still fulfill important functions to maintain social bonds and solidarity. In addition to the rituals surrounding gift giving there are numerous ritual elements in collective manifestations of solidarity. Ritualism and the use of symbols serve to unify groups, communities, clans, and nations by providing a

Recognition of the other	Social distance	Motives	Reciprocity	Solidarity
Recognition of the other ↑	Family Friends Neighbors	Affection Equality	**'Gift'** concrete, personal	
	Fellow citizens Strangers	Equality Instrumentality		**Solidarity**
	Group Community Clan Nation	Instrumentality Power	**'Sacrifice'** abstract, anonymous	

FIGURE 9.1. Four dimensions of solidarity.

collective identification. The reason why ritual has not been included in Figure 9.1 is that it does not differentiate in any meaningful way between the various social units on the social distance continuum. Whereas the ways of expressing ritual will be different in the various social units – family rituals are different from the ritualism present in the dynamics of a group or a nation – ritual as such is an aspect of most forms of solidarity. Let me briefly recapitulate the dimensions.

First, recognition of the other's human worth is more likely to occur among family, friends, and neighbors than among fellow citizens and strangers. In larger entities like groups, communities, tribes, and nations the recognition of otherness becomes less likely, in particular as ideological rigidity and group loyalty increase and the threat to self-determination is felt more strongly. The second and third dimensions are social distance and the related solidarity motives. The combinations in Figure 9.1 are ideal types because in practice many exceptions will occur. For instance, affectivity and equality will be most common among near relatives and friends, but considerations of power and instrumentality cannot be excluded. Think of a personal relationship based on power inequality or on mere personal profit seeking and self-interest. Inversely, motives of affection and equality are not the exclusive prerogative of family and friends but can also be present in larger social units. But, in general, instrumentality and power are the more likely motives to occur in groups, larger communities, tribes, and nations. The relationships among fellow citizens and strangers fall in between: equal exchange is possible, but self-interest and power may motivate their actions as well.

The fourth dimension is reciprocity. Reciprocity as exemplified in the gift is more likely within the small units of family, friends, and neighbors where it contributes to establishing the social ties of solidarity. The personal character of the emotions involved and the concrete expression of these in the gift are typical for small-scale social units. Although gift relationships may occur on a larger scale as well, as in big companies giving gifts to political parties, their potential in bringing about social ties is different from the small-scale interpersonal gift giving, and the underlying motives will reflect more self-interest, instrumentality, and power needs than within the smaller units. Although gifts may be impersonal and abstract, the prototypical gift is personal and concrete. Also sacrifice can be personal and take place in the context of a concrete relationship with another human being, but the abstract and anonymous sacrifice in the name of certain group ideals is more characteristic of larger-scale social units.

It has been said before: all solidarities have strengths and weaknesses. Large-scale group solidarity may be useful to develop a group identity, to make one's presence felt, and to attain political and social goals. The power of small-scale solidarity relies on the direct and reciprocal commitment and responsibility, becoming expressed in mutual respect and help. The risks of small-scale interpersonal solidarity are selectivity and exclusion, whereas large-scale group solidarity can lead to the annihilation of personal autonomy, oppression, and bloodshed. Solidarity, like gift giving, while being indispensable to social life, is never entirely without danger.

What could be the value of this theoretical model when looking at contemporary solidarity? Let us choose two problematic examples: civil solidarity (Chapter 8) and the relationship between autochthonous and allochthonous citizens in Western societies (this chapter). Figure 9.1 informs us that anonymous fellow citizens and strangers do not belong to those categories of human beings toward whom solidarity is easily felt and expressed. Still, this solidarity in particular should be promoted, in the first case because the decline in the level of public respect causes serious concern, in the second one because our society faces the immense task of developing a new social connectedness allowing the autochthonous and the allochthonous to live together in harmony and mutual respect. Avoiding the negative aspects of strong internal group solidarity will be a major issue. One of the many lessons we can learn from Durkheim is that forms of societal organization have an impact on solidarity. When looking for solutions for shortcomings in today's solidarity, the gift model may offer a possible direction because it implies a social contract that ties people together through the morality of mutual obligation. It becomes important, then, to find those forms of societal organization that allow the gift model to unfold the best of its powers.

From Organic to Segmented Solidarity

The multifariousness of solidarity precludes any general statement about an increase or decline of solidarity. As the American historian Thomas Bender said, "How many times can community collapse in America?" (1978: 46). Among the many manifestations of solidarity some will always be decreasing, and others increasing in significance or level, making it impossible to give a final assessment on the level of solidarity in a certain society. A phenomenon like solidarity is therefore mainly interesting in its qualitative aspects and dimensions. Just as Durkheim saw a transformation in solidarity from mechanical to organic solidarity in the course of the nineteenth century, a similar change can be perceived at the turn of the twentieth into the twenty-first century.

An essential change compared with solidarity in Durkheim's times is, of course, the rise of the organized, formal solidarity of the welfare state. Whereas in cases of illness, unemployment, or poverty nineteenth-century citizens had to fall back on charity and other forms of mutual assistance and care, at the beginning of the twenty-first century in most Western welfare states (the European more than the American) there exists a reasonably well organized social safety net for those who are not able to care for themselves or provide for their own livelihood. This has diminished the pressure on informal solidarity and thus increased the independence and freedom of citizens. But, in addition, changes have occurred in informal solidarity itself, which cannot be accounted for by the availability of the organized solidarity of the welfare state. In this book we have, for instance, seen that due to various societal transformation processes informal solidarity has become more individualized, abstract, and global, whereas, at the same time, many traditional forms of solidarity have remained. Despite the great variety of expressions of solidarity, a trend may be observed. As noted in Chapter 8, motives based on self-interest and reciprocity have become more prominent in some forms of solidarity, like the assistance offered to people sharing one's fate. This development is possibly related to the increased emphasis on the self and the new assertiveness. We saw the same emphasis return in the developments of civil solidarity, which we tentatively interpreted as indicating a decline in people's capacity to take the imaginary position of another person. On the other hand, we observed that the anonymous solidarity of writing a bank check has increased: autonomous citizens decide themselves if and to which charity they give money, regardless of what others do. Key words are autonomy and independence, or – put differently – a strengthening and reinforcement of the self vis-à-vis others. Although this does not necessarily mean that others are less recognized, this combination does occur, as we have seen in Chapter 8.

This tendency toward growing independence and fortification of the self indicates that the basis of modern solidarity has fundamentally changed. In Chapter 5 we saw that in Durkheim's view the interdependency of citizens for the provision of their needs was the foundation of organic solidarity. In the course of the nineteenth century societal roles and tasks had become more differentiated and, at the same time, functionally more interwoven. The relationships between citizens were characterized by mutual dependency, and forms of social organization were interconnected. At the start of the twenty-first century this interdependency is clearly declining. An important domain where the decreased interdependency becomes visible is work, as Sennett has observed. Indeed, in large, bureaucratic institutions the organizational conditions are not particularly favorable to interdependency and mutual commitment, and feelings of social connectedness will seldom arise. Recognition of personal value is often rare in these settings. One is an anonymous particle doing one's job more or less independently from other particles.

As a consequence of the individualization process, the better social provisions and the increased wealth, modern citizens' societal opportunities and possibilities have increased in a range of domains – education, mobility, relationship forms, and procreation, to mention just a few – and have therefore contributed to their greater autonomy. Due to these developments the significance of people's mutual dependency as a basis for solidarity has greatly diminished, despite statements on the growing impact of the "network society." Seen from Durkheim's functionalist perspective solidarity had an apparent survival value: the continuity of the community was dependent on it. This situation has clearly changed at the end of the twentieth century. Individuals in Western societies are no longer uniting in solidarity because they need one another for their survival (here the welfare state can provide solace) but because they choose to do so themselves. Personal considerations have partly replaced perceived group advantages as determinants of solidarity. Solidarity has become less based on the mutual recognition of desires and needs, and more on voluntariness. As a consequence, solidarity has also become more noncommittal: individuals no longer express their solidarity because they have to, but because they feel free to do so.

Not only have individuals become more independent in their activities, but also the larger segments of society like family, neighborhood, and church – the "organs" in Durkheim's terminology – have come to function more independently from each other due to processes of differentiation and increasing scale. As a consequence cities, villages, quarters, and neighborhoods have become hybrid and fragmented. Families can do without a neighborhood if they like, and neighborhoods do not need families. There is a growing diversity of organizational forms that people use to give shape and meaning to their lives. This applies, for instance, to the variety of religious affinities, each with their own place to pray, but also to the fields of leisure and social services. For all these fields the principle holds: everyone to his or her own liking. The mosque and the Protestant church exist alongside each other in the same neighborhood, each serving their own group of believers. Similarly, alternative and regular circuits of health care services lead their own independent existence, and on each conceivable domain – sports, volunteer work, theater, film, music – there is a multitude of organized and nonorganized opportunities to spend one's free time. Many sorts of labor have become less tied to a specific urban or regional area. Worldly contacts, whether oriented to work or of a private nature, have become context-independent and can, in principle, be realized from behind any desk with a computer. The different, formal and informal, organizational frameworks of human activity have become less interwoven. They no longer form an "organic" whole from which solidarity arises automatically, as it were, but have become independent, autonomously functioning segments.

In brief, both individuals and forms of social organization in which individuals function have come to stand apart. The basis of solidarity is no longer organic in the Durkheimian sense but has grown independent. One might therefore describe the ongoing change as a transformation from organic to "segmented" solidarity: separate, autonomous segments, connecting (if at all) with other segments no longer out of necessity and mutual dependency but on the basis of voluntariness. The segmented solidarity differs both from Durkheim's mechanical and his organic solidarity. Whereas the "homogeneous segments" of mechanical solidarity were based on mutual likeness and congruence between individual and group identity, the segments on which contemporary solidarity rests are not homogeneous anymore but characterized by diversity and plurality. We still have families, neighborhoods, and churches, but their internal variety is greater than ever. Also the connection between the various social segments has become more loose and less "organic" as we have seen.

As in Durkheim's times it is not the case that segmented solidarity has entirely substituted organic solidarity. The distinction is analytical in kind, and in reality forms of organic as well as the old mechanical solidarity can still be observed. Family solidarity, for instance, is still alive and kicking as we saw in this book, and in particular where mutual assistance and care within immigrant communities in Western societies are concerned, elements of need and survival are still strongly involved. But generally speaking, in contemporary solidarity the aspect of voluntariness has come to supersede that of necessity. The question is, of course, what are the survival chances of a society that rests predominantly on segmented solidarity. The answer will unfold in the course of the twenty-first century.

References

Appadurai, A. (ed.). 1986. *The Social Life of Things: Commodities in Cultural Perspective.* Cambridge: Cambridge University Press.

Arber, S., and Attias-Donfut, C. (eds.). 2000. *The Myth of Generational Conflict: The Family and State in Ageing Societies.* London: Routledge.

Arendt, H. 1963. *On Revolution.* New York: Viking Press.

1978. *The Life of the Mind.* New York: Harcourt, Brace and World.

Baal, J. van. 1975. *Reciprocity and the Position of Women.* Anthropological Papers. Assen: Van Gorcum.

Bailey, F. G. (ed.). 1971. *Gifts and Poison: The Politics of Reputation.* Oxford: Basil Blackwell.

Barthes, R. 1973. *Mythologies.* London: Paladin.

Baudrillard, J. 1988 [1970]. "Consumer society." In Poster 1988: 45–63.

Bauman, Z. 1997. *Postmodernity and Its Discontents.* Cambridge: Polity Press.

1998. *Globalization: The Human Consequences.* Cambridge: Polity Press.

2001. *The Individualized Society.* Cambridge: Polity Press.

Bayertz, K. (ed.). 1998. *Solidarität: Begriff und Problem* [Solidarity: Concept and problem]. Frankfurt am Main: Suhrkamp.

Beck, U. 1986. *Risk Society: Towards a New Modernity.* London: Sage.

Becker, H. A. 1992. *Generaties en hun kansen* [Generations and their opportunities]. Amsterdam: Meulenhoff.

Becker, H. A., and Hermkens, P. L. (eds.). 1993. *Solidarity of Generations: Demographic, Economic and Social Change, and Its Consequences.* Amsterdam: Thesis.

Bender, T. 1978. *Community and Social Change in America.* New Brunswick, N.J.: Rutgers University Press.

Bengtson, V. L. 1993. "Is the 'Contract across generations' changing?" In Bengtson and Achenbaum 1993: 3–25.

References

2001. "Beyond the nuclear family: The increasing importance of multigenerational bonds." *Journal of Marriage and the Family* 63: 1–16.

Bengtson, V. L., and Achenbaum, A. (eds.). 1993. *The Changing Contract across Generations.* New York: Aldine de Gruyter.

Bengtson, V. L., and Mangen, D. J. 1988. "Family intergenerational solidarity revisited." In Mangen, Bengtson, and Landry 1988: 222–238.

Bengtson, V. L., and Roberts, R. E. L. 1991. "Intergenerational solidarity in aging families." *Journal of Marriage and the Family* 53: 856–870.

Bengtson, V. L., Rosenthal, C. and Burton, L. 1990. "Families and aging. Diversity and heterogeneity." In Binstock and George 1990: 263–287.

Bennett, W. 1993. *The Book of Virtues: A Treasury of Great Moral Stories.* New York: Simon and Schuster.

Berking, H. 1999. *Sociology of Giving.* London: Sage.

Binstock, R., and George, L. (eds.). 1990. *Handbook of Aging and Social Sciences.* 3rd ed. New York: Academic Press.

Blau, P. M. 1964. *Exchange and Power in Social Life.* New York: Wiley.

Blieszner, R., and Bedford, V. H. (eds.). 1995. *Handbook of Aging and the Family.* Westport, Conn.: Greenwood Press.

Boszoemenyi-Nagy, I., and Spark, G. M. 1973. *Invisible Loyalties.* New York: Brunner/Mazel.

Bott, E. 1957. *Family and Social Network.* New York: Free Press.

Bourdieu, P. 1984 [1979]. *Distinction: A Social Critique of the Judgement of Taste.* London: Routledge and Kegan Paul.

1990 [1980]. *The Logic of Practice.* Cambridge: Polity Press.

Brink, G. van den. 2001. *Agressieve jongeren. Over jeugd, agressie en beschaving in Nederland* [Aggressive youngsters: On youth, aggression and civility in the Netherlands]. Nijmegen: SUN.

2002. *Mondiger of moeilijker? Een studie naar de politieke habitus van hendedaagse burgers* [More emancipated or more difficult? A study into the political habitus of contemporary citizens]. The Hague: Sdu Publishers.

Brown, R. 1986. *Social Psychology.* New York: Free Press.

Cahoone, L. 2000a. "Civic meetings, cultural meanings." In Rouner 2000: 40–65.

2000b. "Response to Alan Wolfe." In Rouner 2000: 142–151.

Caplow, T. 1982a. *Middletown Families.* Minneapolis: University of Minnesota Press.

1982b. "Christmas gifts and kin networks." *American Sociological Review* 47: 383–392.

1984. "Rule enforcement without visible means: Christmas giving in Middletown." *American Journal of Sociology* 89: 1306–1323.

Carrier, J. G. 1995. *Gifts and Commodities. Exchange and Western Capitalism since 1700*. London: Routledge.

Carter, S. L. 1998. *Civility: Manners, Morals and the Etiquette of Democracy*. New York: Basic Books.

Castells, M. 1996. *The Rise of Network Society*. Oxford: Blackwell.

Cheal, D. 1983. "Intergenerational family transfers." *Journal of Marriage and the Family* 45: 805–813.

——— 1986. "The social dimensions of gift behavior." *Journal of Social and Personal Relationships* 3: 423–493.

——— 1987. "Showing them you love them: Gift giving and the dialectic of intimacy." *Sociological Review* 35: 150–169.

——— 1988. *The Gift Economy*. London: Routledge.

Cohen, R., and Rai, S. M. (eds.). 2000. *Global Social Movements*. London: Athlone Press.

Coleman, J. 1986. *Individual Interests and Collective Action*. Cambridge: Cambridge University Press.

——— 1990. *Foundations of Social Theory*. Cambridge, Mass.: Harvard University Press.

Coleman, J., and Fararo, T. (eds.). 1992. *Rational Choice: Advocacy and Critique*. London: Sage.

Coser, L. A. 1971. *Masters of Sociological Thought: Ideas in Historical and Social Context*. New York: Harcourt Brace Jovanovich.

Coser, L. A., and Rosenberg, B. (eds.). 1965. *Sociological Theory*. New York: Macmillan.

Corrigan, P. 1997. *The Sociology of Consumption*. London: Sage.

Daal, H. J. van. 1994. "Hedendaags vrijwilligerswerk: gedaanten, identiteit en aantrekkingskracht" [Contemporary volunteer work: Forms, identity and attractivity]. In SCP-Report 1994b: 201–217.

Davis, J. 1996. "An anthropologist's view of exchange." *Social Anthropology* 4 (3): 213–226.

Dawkins, R. 1976. *The Selfish Gene*. Oxford: Oxford University Press.

Dekker, P. (ed.). 1999. *Vrijwilligerswerk vergeleken* [Volunteer work compared]. The Hague: Sdu Publishers.

——— 2000. "Sociale en politieke participatietrends" [Trends in social and political participation]. In Ester, van Houten, and Steijn 2000: 63–78.

——— 2002. *De oplossing van de civil society. Over vrijwillige associaties in tijden van vervagende grenzen* [The solution of the civil society: On voluntary associations in times of blurring boundaries]. The Hague: Sociaal en Cultureel Planbureau.

Doreian, P., and Fararo, T. (eds.). 1998. *The Problem of Solidarity: Theories and Models*. Amsterdam: Gordon and Breach.

References

Douglas, M. 1990. Foreword to M. Mauss, *The Gift: The Form and Reason for Exchange in Archaic Societies*, pp. vii–xviii. London: Routledge.

Douglas, M., and Isherwood, B. 1979. *The World of Goods: Toward an Anthropology of Consumption*. London: Allen Lane.

Durkheim, E. 1951 [1897]. *Suicide*. New York: Free Press.

   1964a [1893]. *The Division of Labor in Society*. New York: Free Press.

   1964b [1895]. *The Rules of Sociological Method*. New York: Free Press.

   1965 [1912]. *The Elementary Forms of the Religious Life*. New York: Free Press.

Dykstra, P. 1997. "Employment and caring." NIDI, Working Paper, November.

Dykstra, P. 1998. "Moet de overheid ouderen koesteren? Onze kijk op ouderenzorg" [Should the government cherish the old? Our view on elderly care]. *Demos* 14: 29–31.

Dykstra, P., and de Jong-Gierveld, J. 1997. "Huwelijksgeschiedenis en informele en formele hulp aan ouderen" [Marital history and informal and formal care to the elderly]. *Bevolking en Gezin* 3: 35–61.

Elias, N. 1978. *The Civilising Process*. Oxford: Blackwell.

Elster, J. 1989. *The Cement of Society*. Cambridge: Cambridge University Press.

Emerson, R. W. 1902 [1844]. "Gifts." In *The Works of R. W. Emerson: Essays*, 302–306. London: Grant Richards.

Engbersen, G., Schuyt, K., Timmer, J., and van Waarden, F. 1993. *Cultures of Unemployment: A Comparative Look at Long-Term Unemployment and Urban Poverty*. San Francisco: Westview Press.

Esping-Andersen, G. 1990. *Three Worlds of Welfare Capitalism*. Cambridge: Polity Press.

   1999. *Social Foundations of Postindustrial Economies*. Oxford: Oxford University Press.

Ester, P., van Houten, D., and Steijn, B. (eds.). 2000. *De waan van de dag* [Today's delusions]. Amsterdam: SISWO.

Etzioni, A. 1988. *The Moral Dimension: Toward a New Economics*. New York: Free Press.

Finch, J. 1989. *Family Obligations and Social Change*. Cambridge: Polity Press.

Finch, J., and Mason, J. 1993. *Negotiating Family Responsibilities*. London: Routledge.

Finley, M. I. 1988. *The World of Odysseus*. London: Chatto & Windus.

Firth, R. 1929. *Primitive Economics of the New Zealand Maori*. London: Routledge.

Fiske, A. P. 1991. *Structures of Social Life: The Four Elementary Forms of Human Relations*. New York: Free Press.

Freud, A. 1986 [1936]. *The Ego and the Mechanisms of Defence*. London: Hogarth Press.

Frow, J. 1997. *Time and Commodity Culture: Essays in Cultural Theory and Postmodernity*. Oxford: Clarendon.

Geertz, C. 1973. *The Interpretation of Cultures*. New York: Basic Books.

Gennep, A. van. 1960. *The Rites of Passage*. Trans. by Monika Vizedom and Gabriëlle L. Caffee. London: Routledge and Kegan Paul.

Gilmore, D. D. (ed.). 1987. *Honor and Shame and the Unity of the Mediterranean*. Washington, D.C.: American Anthropological Association.

Girard, R. 1993 [1977]. *La violence et le sacré* [Violence and the sacred]. Paris: Grasset.

Godbout, J. T. 1992. *L'esprit du don* [The spirit of the gift]. Paris: Éditions la Découverte.

Godelier, M. 1999. *The Enigma of the Gift*. Cambridge: Polity Press.

Goffman, E. 1971. *Relations in Public: Micro Studies of the Public Order*. London: Allan Lane.

Gouldner, A. W. 1973a. "The norm of reciprocity: A preliminary statement." In Gouldner 1973c: 226–260.

1973b. "The importance of something for nothing." In Gouldner 1973c: 260–290.

(ed.). 1973c. *For Sociology: Renewal and Critique in Sociology Today*. London: Allen Lane.

Gregory, C. A. 1982. *Gifts and Commodities*. London: Academic Press.

Habermas, J. 1989. Rechtvaardigheid en solidariteit [Justice and solidarity]. In Korthals 1989: 78–109.

Hareven, T. K. 1995. "Historical perspectives on the family and aging." In Blieszner and Bedford 1995: 13–31.

Harris, H. (ed.). 1979. *Scientific Models and Man: The Herbert Spencer Lectures 1976*. London: Oxford University Press.

Hart, J. de. 1999. "Lange-termijntrends in lidmaatschappen en vrijwilligerswerk" [Long-term trends in memberships and volunteer work]. In Dekker 1999: 33–68.

Hechter, M. 1987. *The Principles of Group Solidarity*. Berkeley: University of California Press.

Heider, F. 1958. *The Psychology of Interpersonal Relations*. New York: John Wiley.

Herzfeld, M. 1987. "'As in your own house': Hospitality, ethnography, and the stereotype of the Mediterranean society." In Gilmore 1987: 75–90.

Hochschild, A. 1979. "Emotion work, feeling rules and social structure." *American Journal of Sociology* 85: 551–575.

2000. "Global care chains and emotional surplus value." In Hutton and Giddens 2000: 130–147.

Hoeben, C. 2000. *De organisatie van LETSystemen in Nederland, Vakgroep Sociologie* [The organization of LET systems in the Netherlands]. Groningen: RUG.

Homans, G. F. 1950. *The Human Group*. New York: Harcourt, Brace and World.

References

Honneth, A. 1992. *The Struggle for Recognition: The Moral Grammar of Social Conflicts.* Cambridge: Cambridge University Press.

House, J. S., Umberson, D., and Landis, K. R. (1988). "Structures and processes of social support." *Annual Review of Sociology* 14: 293–318.

Hubert, H., and Mauss, M. 1974. *Sacrifice: Its Nature and Functions.* Chicago: University of Chicago Press.

Hutton, W., and Giddens, A. (eds.). 2000. *On the Edge: Living with Global Capitalism.* London: Jonathan Cape.

Hyde, L. 1983 [1979]. *The Gift: Imagination and the Erotic Life of Property.* New York: Random House.

Inglehart, R. 1977. *The Silent Revolution: Changing Values and Political Styles among Western Publics.* Princeton: Princeton University Press.

Ignatieff, M. 1993. *Blood and Belonging: Journeys into the New Nationalism.* London: Chatto & Windus.

Johnson, C. 2000. "Perspectives on American kinship in the later 1990s." *Journal of Marriage and the Family* 62: 623–639.

Jong-Gierveld, J. de, and van Solinge, H. 1995. "Ageing and its consequences for the socio-medical system." Straatsburg: Council of Europe Press Population Studies 29.

Kecskemeti, P. (ed.). 1952. *Essays in the Sociology of Knowledge.* New York: Oxford University Press.

Keohane, R. O., and Ostrom, E. (eds.). 1995. *Local Commons and Global Interdependence.* London: Sage.

Kertzer, D. I. 1988. *Ritual, Politics, and Power.* New Haven: Yale University Press.

Klein, M. 1987a [1946–1963]. *Envy and Gratitude and Other Works, 1946–1963.* Vol. 3. London: Hogarth Press and Institute of Psycho-Analysis.

   1987b [1957]. "Envy and gratitude." In Klein 1987a: 176–236.

   1987c [1963]. "On the sense of loneliness." In Klein 1987a: 300–314.

Knijn, T., and Komter, A. (eds.). 2003. *Solidarity between the Sexes and the Generations: Transformations in Europe.* Cheltenham: Edward Elgar Publishing.

Kohli, M. 1999. "Private and public transfers between generations: Linking the family and the state." *European Societies* 1: 81–104.

Komter, A. E. (ed.). 1996a. *The Gift: An Interdisciplinary Perspective.* Amsterdam: Amsterdam University Press.

   1996b. "Reciprocity as a principle of exclusion." *Sociology* 30: 299–316.

   2000. "Een kwestie van evenwicht" [A matter of balance]. *Tijdschrift voor de Sociale Sector* 4: 36–39.

   2001. "The disguised rationality of solidarity: Gift giving in informal relations." *Journal of Mathematical Sociology* 25: 385–402.

Komter, A. E., Burgers, J., and Engbersen, G. 2000. *Het cement van de samenleving; een verkennende studie naar solidariteit en cohesie* [The cement of society: An exploratory study of solidarity and cohesion]. Amsterdam: Amsterdam University Press.

Komter, A., and Schuyt, C. J. M. 1993a. Geven in Nederland [Gift giving in the Netherlands]. Amsterdam: Dagblad Trouw.

1993b. "Geschenken en relaties" [Gifts and relationships]. *Beleid & Maatschappij* 20: 277–285.

Komter, A. E., and Vollebergh, W. 1997. "Gift giving and the emotional significance of family and friends." *Journal of Marriage and the Family* 59 (August): 747–757.

2002. "Solidarity in Dutch families: Family ties under strain?" *Journal of Family Issues* 23 (2): 171–189.

Kopytoff, I. 1986. "The cultural biography of things: Commoditization as process." In Appadurai 1986: 64–91.

Korthals, M. (ed.). 1989. *De nieuwe onoverzichtelijkheid en andere opstellen* [The new disorder and other essays]. Meppel/Amsterdam: Boom.

Kulis, S. 1992. "Social class and the locus of reciprocity in relationships with adult children." *Journal of Family Issues* 13: 482–504.

Künemund, H., and Rein, M. 1999. "There is more to receiving than needing: Theoretical arguments and empirical explorations of crowding in and crowding out." *Ageing and Society* 19: 93–121.

Lane, R. F. 2000. *The Loss of Happiness in Market Democracies.* New Haven: Yale University Press.

Lasch, C. 1977. *Haven in a Heartless World.* New York: Norton.

1979. *The Culture of Narcissism: American Life in an Age of Diminishing Expectations.* New York: Warner Books.

Laslett, P. 1971. *The World We Have Lost.* New York: Scribner's.

Lazarus, R. S., and Lazarus, B. N. 1994. *Passion and Emotion: Making Sense of Our Emotions.* New York: Oxford University Press.

Leer, M. van. 1995. "Van honingcoeck tot lingerie. Sinterklaasgeschenken als spiegel van relaties" [From honey cake to lingerie: St. Nicholas gifts as a mirror of relationships]. *Psychologie & Maatschappij* 72 (3): 209–219.

Lévi-Strauss, C. 1961 [1949]. *The Elementary Structures of Kinship.* Trans. J. H. Bell, J. R. von Sturmer, and R. Needham. Rev. ed. Boston: Beacon.

1965. "The principle of reciprocity." In Coser and Rosenberg 1965: 84–94.

1966 [1962]. *The Savage Mind.* Chicago: University of Chicago Press.

Liefbroer, A., and Dykstra, P. 2000. *Levenslopen in verandering. Een studie naar ontwikkelingen in de levenslopen van Nederlanders geboren tussen 1900 en 1970*

References

[Changing lives: A study on life course changes of the Dutch 1900–1970 birth cohorts]. The Hague: Sdu Publishers.

Lindenberg, S. 1998. "The microfoundations of solidarity: A framing approach." In Doreian and Fararo 1998: 61–112.

Luescher, K., and Pillemer, K. 1998. "Intergenerational ambivalence: A new approach to the study of parent-child relations in later life." *Journal of Marriage and the Family* 60: 413–425.

Lukes, S. 1973. *Emile Durkheim: His Life and Work. A Historical and Critical Study.* London: Allen Lane.

Malinowski, B. 1950 [1922]. *Argonauts of the Western Pacific.* London: Routledge and Kegan Paul.

Mangen, D. J., Bengtson, V. L., and Landry, P. H. (eds.). 1988. *Measurement of Intergenerational Relations.* Newbury Park, Calif.: Sage.

Mannheim, K. 1952 [1928]. "The problem of generations." In Kecskemeti 1952: 110–158.

Mauss, M. 1990 [1923]. *The Gift: The Form and Reason for Exchange in Archaic Societies.* London: Routledge.

Mayhew, L. 1971. *Society: Institutions and Activity.* New York: Columbia University Press.

McClellan, A. 2000. "Beyond courtesy." In Rouner 2000: 78–94.

McCracken, G. 1990. *Culture and Consumption.* Bloomington: Indiana University Press.

Mead, G. H. 1962 [1934]. *Mind, Self, and Society.* Chicago: University of Chicago Press.

Merton, R. 1968. "The Matthew effect in science." *Science* 6 (January): 56–63.

Miller, D. (ed.). 1995a. *Acknowledging Consumption: A Review of New Studies.* London: Routledge.

1995b. "Consumption and commodities." *Annual Review of Anthropology* 24: 141–61.

(ed.). 1998. *Material Cultures: Why Some Things Matter.* London: Ucl-Press.

Misztal, B. 1996. *Trust in Modern Societies.* Cambridge: Polity Press.

2001. *Informality: Social Theory and Contemporary Practice.* London: Routledge.

Mutran, E., and Reitzes, D. C. 1984. "Intergenerational support activities and well-being among the elderly: A convergence of exchange and symbolic interaction perspectives." *American Sociological Review* 49: 117–130.

Oorschot, W. van, Komter, A., Houtman, D., and Halman, L. 2001. "Wij en Zij in Europa. De solidariteit van Nederlanders in Europees perspectief" [Us and them; The solidarity of the Dutch in European perspective]. Utrecht: AWSB-papers.

Ogletree, T. W. 1985 [1946]. *Hospitality to the Stranger: Dimensions of Moral Understanding.* Philadelphia: Fortress Press.

Osteen, M. (ed.). 2002. *The Question of the Gift: Essays across Disciplines*. London: Routledge.

Ostrom, E. 1995. "Constituting social capital and collective action." In Keohane and Ostrom 1995: 125–160.

Otnes, C., and Beltramini, R. F. (eds.). 1996. *Gift Giving: A Research Anthology*. Bowling Green, Ohio: Bowling Green State University Press.

Pahl, R. E. 1984. *Divisions of Labour*. Oxford: Basil Blackwell.

Parsons, T. 1952. *The Social System*. London: Tavistock.

1977. *The Evolution of Societies*. Englewood Cliffs, N.J.: Prentice-Hall.

Peristiany, J. G. (ed.). 1968. *Contributions to Mediterranean Sociology*. The Hague: Mouton.

Pessers, D. 1999. "Liefde, solidariteit en recht; Een interdisciplinair onderzoek naar het wederkerigheidsbeginsel" [Love, solidarity, and the law: An interdisciplinary study of the principle of reciprocity]. Ph.D. diss. Amsterdam.

Pitt-Rivers, J. 1968. "The stranger, the guest and the hostile host. Introduction to the study of the laws of hospitality." In Peristiany 1968: 13–31.

Popenoe, D. 1988. *Disturbing the Nest: Family Change and Decline in Modern Societies*. New York: Aldine De Gruyter.

Portes, A., and Sensenbrenner, J. 1993. "Embeddedness and immigration: Notes on the social determination of economic action." *American Journal of Sociology* 98: 1320–1350.

Poster, M. (ed.). 1988. *Selected Writings*. Cambridge: Polity Press.

Putnam, R. 2000. *Bowling Alone: The Collapse and Revival of American Community*. New York: Simon and Schuster.

Raub, W. 1997. *Samenwerking in duurzame relaties en sociale cohesie* [Cooperation in durable relationships and social cohesion]. Amsterdam: Thesis.

Raub, W., and Weesie, J. 2000. "The management of matches: A research program on solidarity in durable social relations." *Netherlands Journal of Social Sciences* 36 (1): 71–89.

Regt, A. de, 1993. *Geld en gezin. Financiële en emotionele relaties tussen gezinsleden* [Money and the family: Financial and emotional relationships between family members]. Amsterdam: Boom.

Roberts, R. E. L., Richards, L. N., and Bengtson, V. L. 1991. "Intergenerational solidarity in families: Untangling the ties that bind." *Marriage and Family Review* 16: 11–46.

Rosenthal, C. J. 1985. "Kinkeeping in the familial division of labor." *Journal of Marriage and the Family* 47: 965–974.

Rossi, A., and Rossi, P. 1990. *Of Human Bonding: Parent-Child Relations across the Life Course*. New York: Aldine de Gruyter.

Rouner, L. S. (ed.). 2000. *Civility*. Notre Dame, Ind.: University of Notre Dame Press.

References

Ryff, C. D., and Seltzer, M. M. 1995. "Family relations and individual development in adulthood and aging." In Blieszner and Bedford 1995: 95–114.

(eds.). 1996. *The Parental Experience in Midlife.* Chicago: University of Chicago Press.

Sahlins, M. 1972. *Stone Age Economics.* London: Tavistock.

Salomon, L. M. 1992. *America's Nonprofit Sector: A Primer.* New York: Foundation Center.

Schudson, M. 2000. *The Good Citizen: A History of American Civic Life.* Cambridge, Mass.: Harvard University Press.

Schuyt, T. 2001. *Geven in Nederland 2001; Giften, legaten, sponsoring en vrijwilliger- swerk* [Giving in the Netherlands: Gifts, legacies, sponsoring, and volunteer work]. Houten/Diegem: Bohn Stafleu Van Loghum.

Schwartz, B. 1967. "The social psychology of the gift." *American Journal of Sociology* 73: 1–11.

1993. "Why altruism is impossible . . . and ubiquitous." *Social Service Review* 67: 314–343.

1996 [1967]. "The social psychology of the gift." In Komter 1996a: 69–80.

SCP-Report. 1994a. *Informele zorg. Een verkenning van huidige en toekomstige on- twikkelingen* [Informal care: An exploration of contemporary and future developments]. Rijswijk: Sociaal en Cultureel Planbureau/VUGA.

1994b. *Civil Society en vrijwilligerswerk I* [Civil society and volunteer work]. Rijswijk: Sociaal en Cultureel Planbureau/VUGA.

1998. *25 jaar sociale verandering* [25 years of social change]. Rijswijk: Sociaal en Cultureel Planbureau/VUGA.

2000. *Nederland in Europa* [The Netherlands in Europe]. The Hague: Sociaal en Cultureel Planbureau.

2002. *Zekere banden. Sociale cohesie, leefbaarheid en veiligheid* [Secure ties: Social cohesion, livability, and security]. The Hague: Sociaal en Cultureel Planbureau.

Sen, A. 1979. "Rational fools: A critique of the behavioral foundations of economic theory." In Harris 1979: 1–25.

Sennett, R. 1998. *The Corrosion of Character: The Personal Consequences of Work in the New Capitalism.* New York: W. W. Norton.

Shils, E. 1991. "The virtue of civil society." *Government and Opposition* 26 (10): 3–20.

Shurmer, P. 1971. "The gift game." *New Society* 18: 1242–1244.

Simmel, G. 1908. *Soziologie: Untersuchungen ueber die Formen der Vergesellschaf- tung* [Sociology: Researches into the forms of sociation]. Leipzig: Dunker und Humblot.

1950 [1908]. "Faithfulness and gratitude." In Wolff 1950: 379–396.

1978 [1907]. *The Philosophy of Money.* London: Routledge.

Smith, A. 2002 [1759]. *The Theory of Moral Sentiments*. Cambridge: Cambridge University Press.

Smith, J., Chatfield, C., and Pagnucco, R. (eds.). 1997. *Transnational Social Movements and Global Politics*. Syracuse: Syracuse University Press.

Sociale en culturele verkenningen. 1999. [Social and cultural explorations]. The Hague: Elsevier.

Strathern, M. 1988. *The Gender of the Gift*. Berkeley: University of California Press.

Straus, V. 2000. "Making peace." In Rouner 2000: 229–247.

Suitor, J. J., Pillemer, K., Keeton, S., and Robison, J. 1995. "Aged parents and aging children: Determinants of relationship quality." In Blieszner and Bedford 1995: 223–243.

Swaan, B. de. 1988. *In Care of the State*. Cambridge: Cambridge University Press.

Titmuss, R. M. 1970. *The Gift Relationship: From Human Blood to Social Policy*. Harmondsworth, Middlesex: Penguin.

Tönnies, F. 1987. *Gemeinschaft und Gesellschaft*. Leipzig: Reisland.

Trivers, R. L. 1971. "The evolution of reciprocal altruism." *Quarterly Review of Biology* 46: 35–57.

Tsvetajeva, M. 2000. *Ik loop over de sterren. Schetsen, dagboekfragmenten en brieven over de Russische Revolutie* [I walk over the stars: Sketches, diary fragments, and letters about the Russian Revolution]. Amsterdam: De Bezige Bij.

Turner, B., and Rojek, C. 2001. *Society and Culture: Principles of Scarcity and Solidarity*. London: Sage.

Turner, V. W. 1969. *The Ritual Process: Structure and Anti-Structure*. Chicago: Aldine.

Uzzi, B. 1997. "Social structure and competition in interfirm networks: The paradox of embeddedness." *Administrative Science Quarterly* 42 (1): 35–67.

Veblen, T. 1934 [1899]. *The Theory of the Leisure Class*. New York: Vanguard Press.

Waal, F. de. 1996. *Good Natured: The Origins of Right and Wrong in Humans and Other Animals*. Cambridge, Mass.: Harvard University Press.

2001. *The Ape and the Sushi Master: Cultural Reflections by a Primatologist*. London: Allen Lane.

Waquant, L., and Wilson, J. 1989. "The cost of racial and class exclusion in the inner city." *Annuals of the American Academy of Political and Social Science* 501: 8–26.

Waldinger, R. 1995. "The 'other side' of embeddedness: A case-study of the interplay of economy and ethnicity." *Ethnic and Racial Studies* 18 (3): 555–580.

Walker, A. (ed.). 1996. *The New Generational Contract: Intergenerational Relations, Old Age and Welfare*. Londen: UCL Press.

Weber, M. 1947 [1922]. *The Theory of Social and Economic Organization*. Trans. by A. M. Henderson and Talcott Parsons. New York: Free Press.

References

Weesie, J., Buskens, V., and Raub, W. 1998. "The management of trust relations via institutional and structural embeddedness." In Doreian and Fararo 1998: 113–139.

Weiner, A. 1976. *Women of Value, Men of Renown: New Perspectives in Trobriand Exchange.* Austin: University of Texas Press.

1992. *Inalienable Possessions: The Paradox of Keeping-while-Giving.* Berkeley: University of California Press.

Wetenschappelijke Raad voor het Regereringsbeleid (WRR). 1999. [Generationally aware policy]. (Report to the government, no. 58 *Generatiebewust beleid*). The Hague: Sdu Publishers.

Willems, L. 1994. "Burgerzin en vrijwillige zorg" [Civic spirit and voluntary care]. In SCP-Report 1994b: 185–199.

Wilson, E. O. 1975. *Sociobiology: The New Synthesis.* Cambridge, Mass.: Harvard University Press.

Wilson, G. 1993. "Intergenerational solidarity from the point of view of people in advanced old age." In Becker and Hermkens 1993: 625–643.

Wispé, L. G. 1972. "Positive forms of social behavior: An overview." *Journal of Social Issues* 28 (3): 1–20.

Wit, T. de, and Manschot, H. (eds.). 1999. *Solidareit* [Solidarity]. Amsterdam: Boom.

Withuis, J. 1990. *Opoffering en heroïek. De mentale wereld van een communistische vrouwenorganisatie in naoorlogs Nederland* [Sacrifice and heroism: The mental world of a communist women's organization in the postwar Netherlands]. Meppel: Boom.

Wolfe, A. 1989. *Whose Keeper? Social Science and Moral Obligation.* Berkeley: University of California Press.

2000. "Are we losing our virtue?" In Rouner 2000: 126–142.

Wolff, K. (ed.). 1950. *The Sociology of Georg Simmel.* New York: Free Press.

Wrong, D. H. 1994. *The Problem of Order: What Unites and Divides Society.* New York: Free Press.

Wuthnow, R. 1991. *Acts of Compassion: Caring for Others and Helping Ourselves.* Princeton: Princeton University Press.

Young, M., and Willmott, P. 1973. *The Symmetrical Family: A Study of Work and Leisure in the London Region.* London: Routledge and Kegan Paul.

Zoll, R. 2000. *Was ist Solidarität heute?* [What is solidarity today?]. Frankfurt am Main: Suhrkamp.

Index

Adorno, T., 51
affection, affectivity, 9, 95, 112, 115, 118,
    120, 124, 161, 162, 190, 191, 199, 201,
    206
    feelings of, 161, 165, 194
aggression, aggressive, 186, 187
    feelings, 186
    tendency to respond with, 186
altruism, altruistic, 80, 84, 85, 109, 111,
    112, 132, 182
    and gift giving, 85
    prescribed, 160, 161, 165, 194
    and selfishness, 118
    and solidarity, 110
    suicide, 204
    surrender, 50
Appadurai, A., 16–17, 31
Arber, S., 164
Arendt, H., 196
assertiveness, 209
    increased, 175
association, 115
    instrumental ties of, 118
asymmetry, 69
    alternating, 86–95, 192
    and power inequality, 190
Attias-Donfut, C., 164
attraction, 115
authoritarian personality, 51
authority, 27, 50, 51, 119
    relational model of, 51
    structures of, 175

authority ranking, 21, 23
autonomy, 92–94, 95, 96–97, 141, 183,
    209, 210
    annihilation of, 207
    desire for, 161
    growing emphasis on, 175
    personal, 175
    women's, 93–94, 192

Baal, J. van, 79
balance of debt, 7, 70–71
Balinese cockfight, 120
barter, 118, 119
Barthes, R., 19
Baudrillard, J., 19
Bauman, Z., 171–172, 178
Bayertz, K., 5
Beck, U., 141, 172
Becker, H., 147
Bender, T., 208
beneficence, norm of, 111
benevolence, acts of, 192
Bengtson, V., 146, 151–152, 153
Bennett, W., 184
Berking, H., 4, 203
blood, 84–85
    and belonging, 201
    donation(s), 3, 20, 36, 84
    loyalty, 201
    sacrifice, 121, 201
Boszormenyi-Nagy, I., 160
Bourdieu, P., 19

Index

Index

Index

Index

Index